Heaven
Bound

OTHER BOOKS AND AUDIO BOOKS
BY LYNN C. JAYNES:

Fast Track to Heaven

Heaven Bound

Speed Bumps On the Way to Perfection

LYNN C. JAYNES

Covenant Communications, Inc.

Cover illustration by Scott Jarrard © Scott Jarrard Illustration Inc. www.scottjarrard.com

Cover design copyrighted 2007 by Covenant Communications, Inc.

Published by Covenant Communications, Inc.
American Fork, Utah

Printed in Canada
First Printing: March 2007

11 10 09 08 07   10 9 8 7 6 5 4 3 2 1

ISBN 978-1-59811-315-0

Introduction

I always believed that time and age dim one's vision. Case in point: my mother came to live with my family in 2000. She had glaucoma and, among other things, was concerned about losing her sight. Though we took Mom to a number of specialists over the years, she lost a good deal of vision in spite of their very competent care. This affected her productivity in several ways. For instance, my family learned to watch our ironed shirts and dresses for brown scorch marks where Mom couldn't see them forming. Mom was great at folding laundry, but no longer so great at matching socks. Mom made delicious pies, but we eventually encouraged her to wait to bake them until someone was home and could read the electronic thermostat on the oven for her. These were minor adjustments for me, but for Mom the adjustments were huge.

Experiences like these only confirmed my belief that time and age diminish vision—physical vision, at least. But there are other kinds of vision: mental and spiritual vision. I know this now because my youngest daughter recently left home for college, and for the first time in my married life I found myself lacking the "vision" to see myself as being very productive. For example, I used to look forward to canning season—if not for the bottled fruit, then at least for the chance to teach my daughters how to do it. But I don't want to bottle anything this year. It's cheaper to buy it, and I have no daughters left to teach. I have no "vision" for being productive, and I'm not yet fifty. That's the part that just does me in: I have half my life left to live, and if I don't do something about it, I will spend those years in the dark.

That's why I'm grateful for Aunt Mae. She had vision well into her golden years. Aunt Mae was able to envision herself as a productive individual despite the handicaps inflicted by time and age.

I remember meeting my Great-Aunt Mae Bean Hinman only once in LaGrande, Oregon. We had gone to LaGrande to visit Aunt Mae's sister, my grandmother, Erma Bean Chadwick. I recall only what seemed to be a very large back-yard and an elderly woman in a dress. That's it. Nonetheless, I know Aunt Mae had vision because of a talk she gave at a women's conference for the Oregon City Stake on March 9, 1985. A talk like this could only have been written by a woman who had vision to see beyond herself. As you read her words, see if you agree:

"Almost everyone starts life as a single. The time they spend that way—be it long or short—can be wonderfully important. What happens during that first single period can set the tone for the years ahead. Like a wise investment, it can pay dividends and interest for the rest of your life.

"For some of us it happens twice. The best preparation for being able to cope the second time around is to have enjoyed it the first time. If your first single years were well spent, there is a residual benefit. Not that you would want to relive them. But just remembering that once you *did* handle your own affairs, you *did* make your own decisions, you *did* paddle your own canoe all by yourself gives you confidence that you can do it *again* if you have to.

"In my town, most young women remained single for a rather short time. The usual pattern was to graduate from high school, get a job, work a year or two, and then marry the first returned missionary that came your way. To me this was frustrating—and not just because my pretty sister was getting all the best dates. There was a big, wide, wonderful world out there, and nobody but me seemed interested in exploring it!

"When my sister announced her engagement at the age of twenty, I thought, 'How sad.' She had never seen the ocean. She hadn't been to Europe. She had never climbed a mountain. She didn't seem to care that she couldn't ride a horse or ski or skate or hike. She could dance, but she hadn't owned a car. And how was she ever going to experience all these vitally important things once she got married? It would be hard to imagine two more opposite personalities in one family.

"We went our separate ways. She became the model homemaker, wife and mother, civic leader, church worker, General Board member. I entered the working world of the single woman, which for me went on and on. And so did I. I remember one day picking up my mail in Florence, Italy. There was a letter from my sister back home. She said, 'Imagine me addressing a letter to my sister in Florence, Italy! Although knowing you, I might have guessed something like that would happen. But I want you to know I wouldn't trade one of my little tousle-headed boys with their muddy boots for all the scrapbooks you are going to have in your collection.' I thought, 'The poor dear. She hasn't learned a thing. She still doesn't know what she is missing.'

"Well, it took me about sixteen years to work the singleness out of my system. And then there came a time when I was ready to settle down and consider that other career that women are supposed to be good at. When I came to Clackamas County as a newly married woman at the ripe old age of thirty-three, I think I was probably the most contented homemaker this county had ever seen. I was totally committed to the domestic role of wife, mother, and farmhand participating in PTA, Cub Scouts, music lessons, fishing trips, church bazaars, church dinners, and all the rest. I loved every minute of it.

"Now, after more than forty wonderful years, I find myself alone again. I think on the books I am counted as a 'single.' But I don't feel single. I was single once before, and this isn't it. I know I'm not a couple, and I am alone a lot, but there is a difference. This time it is not my choice. I feel that this is a special space of time granted to me in which I can try to catch up, or shape up, and maybe make up for some of the things I have neglected to do. What I do with this time will be very important to me.

"Obviously, I had to have a plan. I remembered a motto I had used in my earlier days. It was *self-reliance, self-improvement.* It had worked well for me the first time around. Why couldn't I dust it off and use it for this new phase of my life? Only this time I wouldn't be planning to go out and explore the world. I just wanted to plan for a few quiet, comfortable, reasonably secure retirement years for an aging lady who wanted very much to be self-reliant.

"As for the self-improvement part, I actually wrote that all down. Every day I would try to do something:
- SPIRITUAL—read scriptures, study the gospel, pray
- PHYSICAL—stay healthy, take a walk
- INTELLECTUAL—avoid getting stuck in a rut, read a good book, keep learning, watch good programs on public television
- CULTURAL—explore the arts, read from those best books, see if I can still read French, practice the organ
- SOCIAL—phone a friend, write a letter, make a visit, do something for somebody

"I'm sure I must have picked up these ideas from some Relief Society class. Who else has such noble thoughts? I kept this little chart on my bed table, and every night I checked off the items on the list. Some nights I checked them all off and I felt wonderful. Other nights I didn't check off any of them, and I still felt wonderful because I felt organized; at least I had a plan that would help me avoid the ruts, and I had sense of direction.

"Well, it took just one phone call to shatter all this. I was reminded that I was a grandmother with a family who had needs, and in the next fifteen months those needs were great. We experienced major surgery involving a young mother of three whose baby was only a year old. Then there was a trip to Europe for the parents of five; the youngest of that group was three years old, and Grandma was in charge. Then we welcomed a northeast baby, making that a family of six. Throw in a couple of Christmases, making a total of five round-trip transcontinental air flights for Grandma—which meant ten times through that airport in Chicago. (Some call it O'Hare, but to me it will always be O'Help.) On one flight we lost an engine and wound up in Denver instead of Chicago. On another, the engine wouldn't start and we abandoned the plane on the ground. On yet another the plumbers and electricians were still trying to thaw out the powder rooms and get the lights to working while the passengers were boarding. Once we landed in a near-hurricane at an undersized airport in Charleston. Twice they lost my luggage.

"With children in the first family ranging from one to five years old and in the second family from three to thirteen (not counting the newborn who came later), this grandma found herself working with precision timing to meet schedules for preschool, basketball practices, school programs (all different ages), and church Christmas dinners and programs, not to mention meeting the school bus each way to accommodate a granddaughter on crutches with a sprained foot.

"All of these comings and goings naturally required transportation, so Grandma had to learn to drive the Honda. A Honda, as you may know, has about five gears and a clutch, all of which have to be coordinated somehow if the engine is to keep running. I had not shifted this kind of gear since our 1937 Buick went out. I'm sure I gave those grandchildren some rides they will never forget. I never once remembered to release the emergency brake until we were back in the garage. The only alternative transportation was the huge twelve-passenger van—just slightly smaller than a school bus, it seemed to me. The streets in that rolling hills section of the city were steep and narrow, which made the van even more hazardous than the Honda with Grandma at the wheel. Every excursion out of the garage was an exercise in faith for us all.

"When I finally returned to my little nest on the hill, home looked so good to me. I was more convinced than ever that what a woman of my age needs most is an atmosphere of peace and tranquility. Lots of tranquility. So once again I went back to my chart and my plan for achieving serenity along with reasonable self-improvement.

"I had been home a couple of weeks when I was invited into the bishop's office. They had a job for me. I was called to be a part-time gospel doctrine teacher. My first reaction was that they had lost my records. You just don't take a woman off the retirement shelf for a job that hard. But they assured me the regular teacher was very good and very dependable and my assignment would be only a sometimes thing, so I agreed. Come to find out, the regular teacher was James Bean. And do you know how little we have seen of him lately?

"As I expected, this was not an easy job. But it did fit rather nicely into my schedule. I could consider it all 'spiritual,' and on the weeks I taught the lesson I could check off a whole week. There would still be a little time to work at being retired.

"Then about two months ago I was tapped on the other shoulder. Would I step into the stake president's office? There, one of the counselors explained there was a call awaiting me, sort of a mission call, he said. Well, this time I knew for sure they had lost my records or hadn't read their handbook, because everybody in the Church knows by now that there is a cutoff age for missionaries, and I was well past that. Hadn't they just sung '76 Trombones' at my last birthday party? The stake president explained that it wasn't that kind of a mission, and that age would make very little difference. This call was to work at the Portland Area Bishops' Storehouse. Now I understood about bishops' storehouses. I had been a Relief Society president once and had handled quite a few bishop's orders in my time. I also knew one might be assigned to scrub potatoes, bag oranges, stock the shelves, and do other types of manual labor. So why not? I was strong. And this assignment would fit right into my chart under 'physical.'

"Well, sisters, of all the places in that vast storehouse where they might have put me, I wound up in a little room with the computer. Into that computer is tabulated every can of beans, every pound of meat or vegetables or fruit, all the milk, the cheese, the eggs, the bread—every item used by all the needy families in about three-fourths of the state of Oregon, southern Washington, and northern California. And who operates that machine? I do. Only I. Henceforth and for the duration of the records of this part of the Church, I shall be known as the 'keypunch operator,' KPO for short. Now I ask you, where but in the Mormon Church could a job of that importance fall into hands like these? It was the scariest job I ever tackled. It still is. Theoretically, the idea of self-reliance is a noble principle, but in this situation it's almost ridiculous. There is never a moment that I'm not painfully aware that I could blow the welfare program right out of the Church if I punch the wrong buttons—keys, I think they are called.

"Furthermore, the work doesn't fit into my schedule where I had thought to put it. First, I put it under 'physical.' It's physically exhausting all right, but it's much more. I tried it under 'intellectual,' but that wouldn't do, either. So I've had to make a new category. I call it 'frantic.' I've also had to update my motto. To *self-reliance* and *self-improvement* I have added *self-preservation.*

"Now, sisters, I don't want to leave the impression that my life is all negative right now. While I don't want to boast, I do believe I have already had some influence on conditions at the storehouse and on the men I work with in the head office. It seems that every time I approach that computer they all become a little more alert, a little more aware, and a LOT more prayerful.

"Now, in conclusion, if all of this could happen to me on my way to a quiet retirement, goodness only knows what your world will be like by the time you get to this age. I would like to offer just one suggestion: If you feel there is ever going to be a time in your life when you will need rest and recuperation, TRY to get it BEFORE you reach the retirement years. Because, believe me, you will need all the energy you can muster just to cope with being single the second time around!"

Bless Aunt Mae. I felt so rejuvenated just reading about her goals as a seventy-seven-year-old woman, I thought it might be a good idea to set my own. Following Aunt Mae's lead, I came up with three categories in which I strive to accomplish something every day: Something Spiritual, Something Physical, and Something of Service. Here's to Aunt Mae and her vision.

Camels in the Desert

See if you can finish these phrases—
A stitch in time . . .
A penny saved . . .
Don't count your chickens . . .
The straw that broke . . .

The tendency with that last phrase is to concentrate on the load of straw that broke the camel's back. How high was it stacked? Two feet? Six feet? One piece of straw is so light-weight that I can have several pieces in my hair without knowing it. So how long did it take for the camel to feel the weight? Five thousand straws? Fifteen thousand? At what point did the camel say to himself, "I'm in trouble here"? At what point did he say, "You're kidding—you're going to put on more straw? No, no, no. I refuse. No more straw—you can't make me"? Do you suppose it was seventeen thousand straws? Eighteen thousand forty-one? Which one was it that finally broke his back?

I find myself doing the same thing. After a few hectic days, weeks, or months, one day I'll be driving somewhere and out of the blue I'll be bawling my head off and thinking, "I just can't do this any more. I cannot prepare one more lesson. I cannot accept one more assignment. I cannot take in one more casserole. No one had even better look at me cross-eyed today." And I have to wonder: just exactly which assignment (or straw) was it that put me over the top? Which casserole broke my back?

I spend way too much time worrying about that casserole—trying to decide how to predict that particular casserole in the future so that other motorists don't gaze at me at the intersections as I sniffle and dab at my eyes and stifle my whimpers. It occurs to me that maybe it's not the straw I should be worrying about. Maybe it's the camel.

Have you ever wondered about that camel? Let's pretend we're all in earth science class together. Consider the camel. Camels are uniquely adapted for their dry desert environment. Camels can also exist on bones, seeds, and thorny shrubs. That would be something equivalent to eating the cardboard cereal box. You and I would probably look at those things and declare the beginning of a new diet. You've probably heard that camels can go for days without drinking water. You probably also heard they store water in their humps. I'm told that's not exactly true, but there's more truth to it than one might expect. When camels drink (and when we talk "drink" here, we're talking move-over-at-the-trough-and-get-out-of-my-way-or-be-knocked-over), they can consume up to twenty-one gallons in ten minutes. Their blood cells can expand to 250 percent of their normal size to retain this water. Yours and mine can only expand to 100 percent of their normal size before they would burst and literally drown us. Hence, when a camel has plenty of water his hump is firm. When he has depleted the store of water in his cells, his hump is less firm and may even droop a bit.

A camel retains water so efficiently that its feces can be used for fuel the minute they hit the ground. A camel can retain water so well that its urine can actually be the consistency of syrup. (And I guarantee that detail will keep little boys awake during an entire family home evening lesson.)

When a camel wants to cool itself in the desert sun, it will actually lay against other camels; as their bodies touch, their body temperatures drop. This is quite unlike humans. On a hot summer day while traveling in a car without air-conditioning, the last thing you want to do is touch another human being.

Another unique adaptation of nature is that camels have feet that spread snowshoe-style to keep them from sinking in the sand. If they didn't, it would be the equivalent of you and me wearing stilettos in wet grass. Camels even develop leathery patches of skin on their knees to counteract the abrasive sand. They're amazing, really. So uniquely adapted.

I wonder if all these years I haven't been worrying about the wrong thing: the straw—fitting in family home evening and family scripture study and personal scripture study and personal and family prayers, paying tithing, going to auxiliary training meetings, making sure the kids get to seminary on time, making sure the boys have an ironed shirt for Sunday, wondering whether to leave a sacrament meeting to go to the bathroom, worrying about whether to sing in the ward choir. I've been wondering whether I sit in the church hallway for a few minutes' peace if I will have trouble renewing my temple recommend. I've been trying to figure out whether I should put a little more effort into genealogy, whether I should make more trips to the temple, how to get the family fed before I zip off to Enrichment Meeting or to Sister So-and-So's for visiting teaching, how many more times I must put my name on the sign-up list for missionary meals to get into the celestial kingdom, and how I can fit that all somewhere in my load.

Maybe all this time I should have been worrying about the camel: me. Maybe if the camel were strong, the load wouldn't be the problem. The stronger the camel, the bigger load it can carry. Maybe I have neglected the camel.

I believe that, like the camel, sisters are uniquely adapted for the latter days. I believe that we are uniquely adapted to raise a generation of people prepared to meet Christ. I believe that we have unique qualities and opportunities to help us in our travel through the desert of mortality. Yes, I even think we've eaten a bone or two or a thorny shrub in our day. I know my spirit has been pricked a time or two, and occasionally I've had to swallow hard and distasteful things.

I've given careful consideration to Aunt Mae's plan for self-improvement. I think Aunt Mae knew about strengthening camels. If I'm going to strengthen my camel for the mortality trip, I will daily do something spiritual.

"There cometh a woman of Samaria to draw water: Jesus saith unto her, Give me to drink.

"(For his disciples were gone away unto the city to buy meat.)

"Then saith the woman of Samaria unto him, How is it that thou, being a Jew, askest drink of me, which am a woman of Samaria? for the Jews have no dealings with the Samaritans.

"Jesus answered and said unto her, If thou knewest the gift of God, and who it is that saith to thee, Give me to drink; thou wouldest have asked of him, and he would have given thee living water.

"The woman saith unto him, Sir, thou hast nothing to draw with, and the well is deep: from whence then hast thou that living water?

"Art thou greater than our father Jacob, which gave us the well, and drank thereof himself, and his children, and his cattle?

"Jesus answered and said unto her, Whosoever drinketh of this water shall thirst again:

"But whosoever drinketh of the water that I shall give him shall never thirst; but the water that I shall give him shall be in him a well of water springing up into everlasting life." (John 4:7–14.)

Doing something spiritual will enlarge my capacity because I "shall never thirst." It will hydrate my spirit so that my "hump" doesn't droop.

I will also ensure the capacity of my camel by doing something physical every day. In response to living the Word of Wisdom, the Lord promises:

"And all saints who remember to keep and do these sayings, walking in obedience to the commandments, shall receive health in their navel and marrow to their bones;

"And shall find wisdom and great treasures of knowledge, even hidden treasures;

"And shall run and not be weary, and shall walk and not faint.

"And I, the Lord, give unto them a promise, that the destroying angel shall pass by them, as the children of Israel, and not slay them. Amen." (D&C 89:18–21.)

My camel needs to be able to run and not be weary, walk and not faint. And in addition to good diet and abstaining from harmful substances, I must:

"Cease to be idle; cease to be unclean; cease to find fault one with another; cease to sleep longer than is needful; retire to thy bed early, that ye may not be weary; arise early, that your bodies and your minds may be invigorated." (D&C 88:124.)

No matter how well-fed and -watered, if I am not conditioned for the trip, I cannot succeed in crossing the desert.

The third thing I will do daily to invigorate my camel is to do something of service.

"So when they had dined, Jesus saith to Simon Peter, Simon, son of Jonas, lovest thou me more than these? He saith unto him, Yea, Lord; thou knowest that I love thee. He saith unto him, Feed my lambs.

"He saith to him again the second time, Simon, son of Jonas, lovest thou me? He saith unto him, Yea, Lord; thou knowest that I love thee. He saith unto him, Feed my sheep.

"He saith unto him the third time, Simon, son of Jonas, lovest thou me? Peter was grieved because he said unto him the third time, Lovest thou me? And he said unto him, Lord, thou knowest all things; thou knowest that I love thee. Jesus saith unto him, Feed my sheep." (John 21:15–17.)

It's awfully difficult to think of my burning feet in the sands of mortality when I am concerned with how everyone else is doing. And so—like the camel—when I concern myself with the needs of others and how to get closer to them, it actually invigorates my own energy and cools me from the heat of the day. In serving someone else, I actually increase my own capacity to carry my own load. (Think about that the next time you think you have no time or energy to go visiting teaching.)

It's a whole lot easier for me to remember to do three things every day—something spiritual, something physical, and something of service—than it is for me to worry about the straw. It's truly exhausting and overwhelming to try to keep track of the straw—or wonder how much more I can handle, whether our family scripture study is adequate, if my personal scripture study and personal and family prayers are sufficient, whether I can make it to one more auxiliary training meeting, whether the kids get to seminary on time, whether the boys have ironed shirts for Sunday, and whether leaving a sacrament meeting to go to the bathroom will keep me out of the celestial kingdom. Who has time for that kind of worry?

"Therefore, dearly beloved brethren, let us cheerfully do all things that lie in our power; and then may we stand still, with the utmost assurance, to see the salvation of God, and for his arm to be revealed." (D&C 123:17.)

Perhaps it's time to forget the straw, strengthen myself, and then "stand still, with the utmost assurance, to see the salvation of God. . . ." He will help me carry whatever load is necessary for the journey.

Something Spiritual

Earthquake, Wind, and Fire

My daughter Rachel ran track for four years. She did well, worked hard, and had a lot of success. She qualified for and medaled at state competitions for three years in a row, and planned to go again the fourth year. For the first three years, Rachel had a coach whose sum total of advice was, "Run hard. Turn left." Rachel did pretty well on that advice. Sure, she worked on form and handoffs and starts, but when it came right down to it, her coach's advice was still, "Run hard. Turn left."

The fourth year, Rachel had a new head track coach who had new ideas. He wanted to start the kids on a training program based on research designed to help them peak at exactly the right time. Some athletes, as you know, peak too early in the season—midway through or three-quarters of the way through. Some peak after the season is over. So the coach started Rachel and the other kids on this new training program. All of a sudden the distraction of this new training complicated Rachel's track season. She was a few days past the district tournament and felt like she was still waiting to peak. She had posted some strong times, but hadn't been consistent and didn't feel like she had yet reached her potential. She was frustrated.

Life does that. It throws out little distractions—and if we don't conquer them, they become complications. It's like the experience I had picking asparagus with my three-year-old grandson. I took Austin out to pick asparagus because my mother picked it, I picked it, my kids picked it, and now it was his turn. I took him to a great little asparagus ditch bank. (And noooo, I'm not going to tell you where it is. Hunters protect hunting spots, fishermen protect fishing holes, and I'm protecting my asparagus ditch. However, in the spirit of the law of consecration, I'll share my *asparagus* with you . . . just not my ditch.)

We came to the first batch of asparagus and I showed Austin how to break off the asparagus without pulling it up. He thought this was great. He didn't understand why we would pick something he didn't like, but he thought hunting it was fun.

He did well until we came to the ditch. This ditch was not a little feed ditch at the top of the field, but a lateral from the canal, and a lot of water was running through it. Austin looked at the water and asked, "Grandma, can I have a drink of that water?"

I answered, "No, Austin, it's dirty."

"Oh, it's dirty?"

"Yes. It's dirty."

"We can't drink it?

"No, we can't drink it."

"Will it make us sick?"

"Yes, it will make us sick." He thought about that.

"Grandma, does the water have cow poopy in it?"

I wondered where he came up with that, then glanced around and saw some cattle corrals in the nearby field. It was a logical explanation.

"Well, probably," I answered.

"Oh, the cow poopy makes the water dirty?"

"Yes, Austin."

We discussed the dirty, cow-poopy water for a good five minutes before we could get back to picking asparagus, but I finally got him on task again. We moved slowly along the ditch, picking asparagus, when we suddenly came across an old dead calf that was nothing but bones and a little hide. AND WE HAD TO DISCUSS THE DEAD COW.

"Grandma, the cow died?"

"Yes, Austin, the cow died."

"Why did it die?"

"Well, it probably just got sick and died."

"Oh." Big pause while he thought about this. "Did it drink the poopy water, Grandma?"

Okay, I guess if you're trying to connect things, that might work. "Yeah, Austin, it probably did."

Austin was fascinated by the cow. We discussed it and examined the bones for a good five or ten minutes. It took forever to get him back on task again, but I finally pulled him away from the distraction and got him picking asparagus again. Then Austin stopped, reached down to pick a sprig of asparagus, and discovered he was standing in an ant pile. Ants were crawling all over his shoes and pants.

"Grandma . . . GRANDMA . . . GRANDMA!"

Suddenly that little three-year-old's life became pretty complicated. I pulled him out of the ant pile, brushed him off, and stood him in a safe place. BUT THEN WE HAD TO DISCUSS THE ANTS.

"Grandma, the ants live there?"

"Yup."

"The ants eat the dead cow?"

"Hmmmm . . . well, probably." (Good point.)

"The cow drink the poopy water and die, and the ants eat it?"

And suddenly he was no longer looking for asparagus. The rest of the morning was a complete waste of time. HE WAS WATCHING OUT FOR THOSE FLESH-EATING ANTS.

That's the way life goes, isn't it? We just get distracted from the goal and we complicate the heck out of life. The prophet Elijah found himself in the same spot. In 1 Kings 19, Elijah has just confounded the priests of Baal by calling down fire out of heaven to consume the altar and sacrifice, which had been drenched by barrels full of water. Still, after that tremendous display of priesthood power, the children of Israel did not heed his warnings. And to complicate matters, Jezebel was trying to find him so she could slay him. So Elijah hid in a cave.

"And he came thither unto a cave, and lodged there; and, behold, the word of the LORD came to him, and he said unto him, What doest thou here, Elijah?

"And he said, I have been very jealous for the LORD God of hosts: for the children of Israel have forsaken thy covenant, thrown down thine altars, and slain thy prophets with the sword; and I, even I only, am left; and they seek my life, to take it away.

"And he said, Go forth, and stand upon the mount before the LORD. And, behold, the LORD passed by, and a great and strong wind rent the mountains, and brake in pieces the rocks before the LORD; but the LORD was not in the wind: and after the wind an earthquake; but the LORD was not in the earthquake:

"And after the earthquake a fire; but the LORD was not in the fire: and after the fire a still small voice." (1 Kgs. 19:9–12.)

It occurs to me, then, that the Lord wanted Elijah to understand that big miracles, big displays of power, would never convert people. If we want to hear the word of the Lord we must listen for the still, small voice.

How will we hear the still, small voice? **Get out of the wind** . . . wind that includes over-scheduled activities, camps, teams, and the wind of taking on too many projects. The

Lord is not in the wind. **Get out of the earthquake** . . . the earthquake of shifting values, shifting fashions, shifting philosophies. The Lord is not in the earthquake. **Get out of the fire** . . . the fire of being overly consumed with ourselves, our lives, our schedules, our wants, and our desires. The Lord is not in the fire. There are plenty of distractions in this life. But if we move beyond the distractions and keep life simple, we'll hear the still, small voice.

I know some young priests who did not get caught up in the wind, the earthquake, and the fire, but who managed instead to listen to the still, small voice. My nephew Seth was born with cerebral palsy. Life for him has been a struggle. He underwent surgery and had braces on his legs before he could learn to walk. He used sign language to communicate before therapists could teach him to use his voice. He struggles with using motor skills—walking, writing, buttoning buttons, and just about everything you can name. But he's a great kid, and people love him—most people. There have been a few who have made fun of him and who have made his challenging life even harder.

When Seth was a senior in high school his family moved into a new ward. His parents were a little apprehensive about how the priests in that ward would accept Seth, but the priests in that quorum were wonderful to him. They accepted him, included him, helped him, and were his friends.

A few months after moving to the new ward, Seth was badly injured in an automobile accident. When the priests in his quorum found out about it, they got together and immediately went to the hospital to see him. That in itself was a great thing to do for Seth, but they didn't stop there. The next night the priests got together again, knelt in prayer, and began a fast for Seth. That's listening to the still, small voice.

What makes their effort even more magnanimous was the fact that some of the priests were seniors and were participating in a track meet the next day. It wasn't just any track meet—it was the district track meet. If they didn't qualify at the district level, they would not advance and be able to compete in the state track meet their senior year. Keep in mind: there isn't a track coach in the world who would recommend fasting on the day of a track meet. At the very least, a coach would expect athletes to stay hydrated and to eat a starchy meal the night before. Yet these priests did not get caught up in the wind of athletic competition, the earthquake of a district track season during their senior year, or the fire of the desire to perform their best. Instead, they listened to a still, small voice and performed a great service for their friend Seth. That's what you and I need to do—quit making life so complicated that we can't hear what the Lord is trying to tell us through the still, small voice.

How do we make life less complicated? Is the advice as simple as, "Run hard. Turn left"? Moses' instructions were pretty simple when he told his people: "And thou shalt love the LORD thy God with all thine heart, and with all thy soul, and with all thy might." (Deut. 6:5.)

Later, the Lord told His disciples the same thing as He recited the first and second great commandments to the lawyers. So keep life simple. Yes, distractions come to everyone, but they only become complications if we allow them to.

We all have burdens to carry. We need them, because they are the things that will ultimately sanctify us and make us strong. The Lord has promised to help us with our burdens—to lighten the load, to make us stronger, or some-times to remove the burden. In addition to our burdens, we also have things we *choose* to carry. Baggage does nothing to strengthen us. You can't give all your heart to God if part of your heart is tied up in anger, jealousy, unrighteous judgment, criticism, envy, or labeling. You can't give your entire soul to God if your soul is competing, comparing, and categorizing.

You can't give all your might to God if your might is tied up in earning money for the luxuries, recreation, and hobbies money can buy.

So carry your burdens, but get rid of your baggage. If we want to simplify our course, we need to avoid what the Lord described as the distractions that would abound just prior to His second coming.

"And Jesus answered and said unto them, Take heed that no man deceive you.

"For many shall come in my name, saying, I am Christ; and shall deceive many.

"And ye shall hear of wars and rumours of wars: see that ye be not troubled: for all these things must come to pass, but the end is not yet.

"For nation shall rise against nation, and kingdom against kingdom: and there shall be famines, and pestilences, and earthquakes, in divers places. . . .

". . .And then shall many be offended, and shall betray one another, and shall hate one another.

"And many false prophets shall rise, and shall deceive many.

"And because iniquity shall abound, the love of many shall wax cold.

"But he that shall endure unto the end, the same shall be saved." (Matt. 24:4–7, 10–13.)

Let's get rid of those distractions like the cumbersome baggage they are. Let's shy away from the kinds of distractions that fouled up Rachel's track training and Austin's asparagus picking. Let's not be distracted by the wind, the earthquake, and the fire—instead, let's keep life simple so that we may be more receptive to the still, small voice.

Creating Moats

Somebody ought to be shot—namely the producers of those home fix-it-up and do-it-yourself shows. They have no idea the number of marriages they've stressed. I should know.

We recently remodeled. Of course, the plan in the beginning was to hire out all the "hard stuff." Right. Like that ever works out. In the past, this plan has always been torpedoed by, "Honey, I think we can do it ourselves and save a lot of money." And that's why at one point a husband—who shall remain nameless, but we'll call him "Fred"—was playing electrician and a lightning bolt shot across the dining room. It convinced me in a hurry that saving money was not the best plan. But Fred? Not so. It took putting a foot through the ceiling and then falling completely through to convince him. He's a slow learner.

Not me—I'm no novice at this any more. I was ready for the torpedo this time, so when we talked recently about remodeling I put my foot down. The electrical work would be hired out, the drywall work would be hired out, and somebody else would construct the staircase and do the finish work—you know, like actually make sure the door will shut without swinging a hip at it. And furthermore, I did not want to hear any of the following:

"Is half an inch close enough?"

"If we don't tell her, she'll never know."

"Can't you just hang a picture over it?"

Or, my favorite: "Shhhh, don't tell Mom."

Our remodeling is done now, and it almost worked. Two out of four isn't bad. However, because I'm *not* a slow learner and because next time I'll be smarter yet, I now intend to have anyone carrying a tool within 200 feet of my house answer a few questions: Explain what the phrase "within half an inch" means to you. Explain what you mean by, "It's good enough for the girls I go with." Or how about this: In order to change out the bathroom stool, which of the following tools would you use?

- Duct tape
- The thingamajig
- The . . . well, you know—the . . . well, it looks kinda like pliers but not
- Anything connected with the words "power tool"

Here's the thing. These men who fumble through remodeling jobs, bungle car mechanics, think that the more stereo wires that show the better the job, build garage shelves out of any material not previously nailed down, and skin up the tree trunks with the lawnmower are the same men we are to sustain as priesthood leaders. Is that mind-boggling to anyone other than me?

My husband tried to build our grandsons a fort this summer. He salvaged some logs from a home that partially burned, dug a trench with the backhoe (because all of his projects must involve a backhoe), stuck the logs end-up in the trench, and tried to tap the logs down. He believed this would work, but he neglected to factor in the eensy-weensy detail that we flood-irrigate our lawn. Following our next irrigation run, the logs fell over and the holes filled up with water. He didn't create a fort—HE CREATED A MOAT. To be honest, the grandkids weren't necessarily disappointed. But a moat is not a fort. And the person who created this moat has the priesthood and could potentially create worlds someday. If he can't tackle a fort, do you really blame me for wondering about his ability to create worlds?

My son Homer and I once had a lively debate about whether I could actually co-exist in the celestial kingdom with priesthood holders like him—you know, him as a priesthood holder, with all his faults, and me with all my . . . I think he used the word "judgments" or something like that. We were engaged in verbal sparring, and I've heard there is no contention allowed in the celestial kingdom, so maybe Homer had a point. Then he said, "Maybe we should just get a time-share condo there." I think this is an excellent idea—we could schedule weeks. This is inspiration! It must be in the scriptures somewhere. Timeshare condos in the celestial kingdom—THIS COULD WORK.

The one flaw, of course, is that it is *not* in the scriptures. I looked. For that matter, I couldn't find a perfect priesthood holder in the scriptures, either, other than the Savior. That started me thinking—and I think I could build a perfect priesthood holder.

The perfect priesthood holder would have a little of Brother Barnes in him. Brother Barnes is kind, humble, and compassionate. The perfect priesthood holder would have a little of Homer in him—the part that strives to be diligent in keeping the commandments, that puts hobbies on the back burner so that he can devote himself to getting an education and providing for a future family, that gives up Mountain Dew to become more obedient. The perfect priesthood holder would have a little of Will's gentleness, a little of Levi's courage in obeying promptings.

The perfect priesthood holder would have Tommy Williams' compassion—the compassion that enabled him to take someone else's ten-year-old girl to a Daddy-Daughter Primary activity and make her feel like she was special. The perfect priesthood holder would have a little of Brother Hugh Baker's dedication to his Sunday School class of fifteen-year-olds. No priesthood leader would be complete without Brother Max Leavitt's discipleship as he calls every student by name and shakes each and every hand.

A great priesthood leader would have a little of my son-in-law Ed's enthusiasm and his appreciation of the arts and his care over what color the kitchen wall is painted (instead of saying, as my husband does, "What's wrong with white?"). A really great priesthood holder would have a little of Grandpa Hoops's endurance and patience in taking grandchildren to a cabin every summer and never losing his temper with them or finding fault with them.

And a really great priesthood leader would have a little of Fred in him—not the moat-building part, of course, but the shepherd part. The part that makes sure everybody's car works, that makes sure lots of the local high school boys have opportunities to earn money, the part that looks for people he can help. The part that looks all around town for a little pantry cupboard for me, but finds they're all too expensive and decides to build me one—which ends up costing more than if he'd originally bought one at the store. And who—most of all—loves me. That would be about perfect.

In the meantime, I recognize that just as Moses needed the support of Aaron and Hur to hold up his arms if the Israelites were to prevail in war, the imperfect priesthood holders in my life also need my supporting hands—not my judgments, not my mouth, and not my sarcasm.

I will do better.

Death of the Natural Man

Sometimes my spirituality wanes. When that happens I try to focus on a single scripture—to tear it apart, analyze its meaning, and compare it to my life. This exercise requires a lot of courage because it exposes me to critical examination—not a pretty sight.

One Sunday I identified one scripture—only one—and tried to live it for just the three hours of Sunday block meetings. Easy, right? Unless, of course, I'm human. The scripture I had chosen was simple:

"For the natural man is an enemy to God, and has been from the fall of Adam, and will be, forever and ever, unless he yields to the enticings of the Holy Spirit, and putteth off the natural man and becometh a saint through the atonement of Christ the Lord, and becometh as a child, submissive, meek, humble, patient, full of love, willing to submit to all things which the Lord seeth fit to inflict upon him, even as a child doth submit to his father." (Mosiah 3:19.)

To launch my experiment, I began with the phrase, "yields to the enticings of the Holy Spirit." According to D&C 11:12, yielding to the Spirit can lead us to do what is right or good. The Spirit can also change our nature so that the desire to sin is replaced with the desire to follow Christ. I felt I had that desire because of thoughts such as, "I want more spirituality. I want more spiritual experiences." So with that desire in my heart, I set out to obtain some spirituality—to gather in some of the Holy Spirit. I was certain the Holy Spirit was out there enticing me already if I could just tune into it.

As with most attempts at self-improvement, I started out with high spirits. I made it through the first two meetings, trying to learn what the Holy Spirit would have me know. But then I sat down in Relief Society and quickly noticed that Sister So-and-So was teaching. My heart fell. There are many different types of learners and just as many different types of teachers. While I was sure this sister was reaching *someone* with her teaching style, I knew it wasn't me. It wasn't so much a problem with her, but rather a problem with me. I already knew the lesson would include a twenty-minute tirade about the evils of the earth, this generation, and where the youth were headed. To me, nothing detracts from the Holy Spirit more than a tirade about the ailments of mortality. But with my scripture in mind, I decided to try extra hard to be positive—to look for the good in the lesson.

The next part of Mosiah 3:19 talks about Saints who "putteth off the natural man." The "natural man" is filled with pride, selfishness, and rebellion against God (see Mosiah 16:5). In order to put off this nature, an individual must repent of his or her sins (see Mosiah 26:29) and submit to the will of God.

Okay, the gloves were off. It was bare-knuckle time. Could I really put off my natural man? Ewww, ick. That requires the "repentance" word. That also requires laying aside the comforts of mortality—like sleep, sarcasm, and reading the Sunday paper instead of preparing for a lesson, to name just a few.

I knew something about the death of the natural man. Not long ago I was asked to take over an early-morning seminary class for the remainder of the year. I cried for a week and two days. It's not that I felt unprepared or unable—I had taught before, and I knew the drill. I cried for the death of the natural man—that part of me that could no longer sleep until seven in the morning but would have to wake up at five thirty and tiptoe around the house so others could sleep while I prepared. I cried because my natural man would have to go to bed by about eight thirty, giving me only about two hours a day with my family after a full day of work. I cried because I would be exhausted most of the time and not have as much energy for my grandchildren. I cried because I would have to give up several hours of sewing and quilting on Saturday—not to mention my nap. I cried because I might never have the time to write or organize my recipes or make my grandson's rag quilt.

It simply meant I would have to "put off" some of my natural man. "Putting off" made it sound way too simple, like I could simply lay it aside as I might a sweater or coat—that perhaps I could pick it up again later when circumstances changed. But deep in my heart I knew it really meant I had to bury the thing—put it to death, embalm it, bury it, and never see it again. Never.

My natural man and I have grown quite close. We're comfortable. We relax in each other's company. We don't mind each other's silence and we don't mind each other's conversation, either. We don't even really care if the other is listening. We don't expect too much of each other, and we're never disappointed. My natural man was my friend. If I was going to have to murder him and then have a funeral for him, I felt he should receive a proper mourning period and a proper burial. Hence, I cried for two days during the denial period, which is the first stage of grief.

Unfortunately, I couldn't afford to stay in denial for long—after all, I had only a week to put this together. So I decided to move right into the shock phase. This involved several pleadings that included phrases such as, "Oh, Heavenly Father, do you realize what you're asking me to give up?" and, "You can't really be serious." He assured me He was. I tried one last ploy—"Heavenly Father, don't you remember all the opposition I faced in my personal life last time I taught seminary? I just can't face that fiery furnace of opposition again. If that's always a part of this assignment, then I just don't have the strength. Please don't ask me to do this." But He did.

And then came the mourning period. I allowed myself a little leeway here. If done properly, grief requires several tissues, several headaches, and several prayers with the exclamation, "Oh, help!" uttered several dozen times. But grief is exhausting, thought-consuming work. Eventually I was so emotionally exhausted that I decided to give up the natural man and bury him simply because I couldn't sustain the grieving period. And no one was bringing me casseroles, ham, and funeral potatoes, so what was the point?

That was the death of the natural man, or at least a part of him. But back to my Sunday experiment. This Relief Society lesson was going to require even more death of the natural man, and I had only about thirty minutes to get my act together. I had already decided to look past the teacher's tirade of the world's evils. However, if I was going to move on, I would have to give up examining her clothes and trying to figure out why she had chosen them. I'd have to ignore the way her upper lip never moved, the way her glasses slid to the bottom of her nose (which invariably made my own nose itch), her haircut, her hair color, her makeup. I could go on and on, but to avoid shaming myself further, I'm hoping you can appreciate how caught up in the superficiality of any situation I can become.

I reminded myself that in order to put off this natural man, an individual must repent of his or her sins and submit to the will of God. So I started my laundry list of things I probably needed to repent of—being too casual in worship and not focusing. Being defiant? Considering myself a better teacher? Ouch.

Next came the injunction to "becometh a saint through the atonement of Christ the Lord." As we humbly accept the Atonement of the Savior, He can remove the effects of sin from us (see Alma 34:8–16) and we can experience a "mighty change . . . in our hearts" (Mosiah 5:2) as we change from our fallen state to a state of righteousness (see Mosiah 27:25).

I knew this would require that I concentrate on the lesson material. I'm a little embarrassed to admit this, but in order to achieve concentration I had to actually look at the floor and not at the teacher.

Then there was the admonition to "becometh as a child, submissive, meek, humble, patient, full of love." We are not asked to be childish, but to become like a child—willing to submit to a righteous Father, willing to do His will instead of our own (see 3 Ne. 11:37–38).

Was I willing to change my focus? Was I willing to ask myself this Sunday morning and every Sunday morning to be open to what God might want me to do instead of just wondering about my own comfort and entertaining my own thoughts? Was I really willing to ask, "What does God want me to do?" I tried to think how this might relate to our Relief Society lesson that Sunday. I tried to decide if the Lord wanted me to sustain the teacher and participate in the lesson, to concentrate on applying the principles to my own life, or what? Ultimately, I did participate. I also spoke to a new ward member after the meeting and found out we had several acquaintances in common—and that she knew absolutely no one in our ward. Had I not been open to God's will, I might have missed this opportunity for friendship.

Let me assure you, I have been a much better student in any classroom of the Church since that time. It was one single scripture, and I tried to live it completely for the space of only three hours. Grueling, simply grueling.

A Cold World

When I was growing up my family raised potatoes on our farm. I had a love/hate relationship with the potato harvest. I loved the homemade French fries; I loved the smell of the dirt as the potatoes were dug out of the ground. I loved autumn and the long, slightly cool days with cobwebs drifting through the fields. I loved the crackle of dead weeds on the ditch bank. It takes a little longer to detail the things I hated . . .

During each potato harvest, my sisters and I came home from school and prepared to help with the harvest. We changed out of our school clothes and put on long underwear, work clothes, two or three sweatshirts, three pairs of socks, and insulated whole-body coveralls over the top of it all. Then came the knit hats and cotton gloves, the bandanas around our noses and mouths, and the plastic safety goggles to complete the ensemble. Once dressed, we were all the same horrendous size, and no one could tell who was who. Then we waddled out to the field to roll onto the spud digger. (And heaven help us if we forgot to go to the bathroom before pulling on the overalls. We only had to make that mistake once!)

The back of the spud digger had a platform just big enough for two and a half people to stand on. If there were three of us on the digger, one had to lean a little precariously over the boom that carried the potatoes into the truck. Our job was to throw off dirt clods, vines, rotten potatoes, dead rabbits, old tennis shoes, license plates, and other debris that came bouncing across the rollers before the spuds went up the boom and into the truck. This was dirty work, and it seemed the smell of water-rot potatoes never truly left our nostrils until a week before Christmas.

Potato harvesting is tricky business. It's necessary to wait for a hard freeze to kill the vines, thicken the skins, and set the sugar in the spuds. But waiting for a hard freeze puts you right up against cold weather. The harvest cannot begin until late morning when the frost leaves the ground and, in our case, doesn't end for the day until the frost again sets in, which is late at night. If the harvest was going well and we didn't have too many equipment problems, we loaded the last truck about nine or nine thirty.

Weather forecasts became extremely important during harvest. The tiniest bit of moisture can make the fields too slick for the equipment. Truthfully, I don't think anyone gave any thought at all to what the weather might do to the workers on the spud digger. The status of the potato itself was paramount. I remember one year we had to leave a few acres of potatoes still in the field—because of the early winter and several equipment breakdowns, we simply could not harvest them. There was no joy in our home that harvest. Our farm was in mourning.

I don't cry too easily. Okay, back up . . . back up. I mean I don't cry easily when in pain. But one fall we were digging spuds and facing the threat of an early winter. We had several equipment breakdowns and things were a little tense, to say the least. I even heard it whispered that it might be another year like the one when we had to leave spuds in the ground. We worked long hours, and for the last week or so of harvest we didn't quit at nine or nine thirty; we worked until eleven or eleven thirty, until the frost made it absolutely impossible to dig any more. Then, half-frozen, we went home, took a quick hot bath, and literally fell into bed to dream all night of spuds bouncing across the rollers. We were tired, hungry, and cold during most of that harvest, but no one dared complain.

At last, there were only a few acres left, but snowstorms were predicted—not the kind of snowstorm that leaves a skiff of snow, but the kind that drives the snow horizontally at about thirty miles an hour, creating a wet environment compounded by the windchill factor. This was it. Whenever that snow hit, it would be our last day of harvest. We were so close.

When my sisters and I went to get on the spud digger that night, we were warned that under no circumstance were we quitting until we absolutely could go no longer. About eight thirty the first snowfall came. It didn't "fall" really—it came like a freight train. Soon the field turned to mud and the loaded trucks had a hard time maneuvering. Finally someone got on a tractor, hooked up to the trucks with a chain, and pulled the trucks through the fields so we could continue digging. It slowed the process considerably, and every minute we stood on the digger exposed to the elements without moving for warmth, the harder it became to warm ourselves when it was time to work again.

Very little dirt was falling through the digger chains—because mud doesn't shake out. My sisters and I worked furiously to pull as much mud from the rollers as we could. It was too dangerous to wear insulated gloves: if our fingers got caught in the rollers, we couldn't pull our hands out of an insulated glove. Instead, we wore the little cotton ones, and they quickly became soaked with the moisture from the mud and snow. My hands felt like clubs. My feet were constantly stinging. We had piled some dirt clods over our feet early in the evening to help insulate them, but the clods were no match for the cold.

I remember this night so clearly because of the stinging pain I felt in my feet and hands. I cannot describe how cold I was. The trucks had heaters and the tractors had heaters, but there was no respite for the workers on the spud digger. I have never been as cold as I was that night. Every time I touched a potato or a mud clod, I let out a little whimper. Eventually my whimpers became sobs. Even though my sisters stood right next to me, I knew they would never hear me crying because of the incredible noise level of the harvesting equipment. So I cried and cried and cried because I was so cold.

That was a long time ago. We did get every last potato out of the field that year, but I have always felt I paid an awful price for it. My feet are always cold. I wear a jacket from the middle of August to the first of July. In Relief Society I often grab a lap quilt from the closet just to get through the meeting. In my mind, I will always blame the spud digger.

But it's much more than the spud digger. In other ways, there is a chill in the world. It's easy to feel the bite of cynicism, sarcasm, and negativity. The world becomes icy at times with an egocentric attitude, indifference, or apathy; you can get downright frostbitten by the lack of faith and abundance of materialism. There are times I've cried because of the harsh, unforgiving coldness in the world that has chilled my soul to its very core.

There is a way, though, to warm our hearts and souls. There is a fire that can thaw a frozen world. The Atonement of Jesus Christ is the fire that invites us to come in from the cold.

Fire has two purposes. It can consume and destroy, but it can also provide light and warmth as it cleanses and purifies. The fire of the Atonement does both, but one is much more pleasant than the other.

First, let's look at the fire that consumes:

"And behold, according to the words of the prophet, the Messiah will set himself again the second time to recover them; wherefore, he will manifest himself unto them in power and great glory, unto the destruction of their enemies, when that day cometh when they shall believe in him; and none will he destroy that believe in him.

"And they that believe not in him shall be destroyed, both by fire, and by tempest, and by earthquakes, and by bloodsheds, and by pestilence, and by famine. And they shall know that the Lord is God, the Holy One of Israel." (2 Ne. 6:14–15.)

This kind of fire scares me. It destroys. I've been burned a time or two by a hot oven or curling iron. It is not pleasant. I don't recommend it.

Next let's look at the fire that provides light and warmth, the fire that is cleansing and purifying. The Lord led the children of Israel in a pillar of fire by night. The Lord also appeared to Moses in a burning bush, but the bush was not consumed. This type of fire does not destroy; it purifies and comforts. It lends light and warmth.

"But, behold, I say unto you, that you must study it out in your mind; then you must ask me if it be right, and if it is right I will cause that your bosom shall burn within you; therefore, you shall feel that it is right." (D&C 9:8.)

This is the kind of fire I want—the fire that can warm me from the harsh coldness of the world. Of this type of fire, Elder Neal A. Maxwell said, "Jesus' glorious Atonement is the central act in all of human history! It provides the universal Resurrection; it makes our personal repentance and forgiveness possible. . . . We are to change our thoughts and then behavior until we are turned away from our sins. . . . Repentance is thus a continuing process in which each of us needs to draw on the Atonement for real relief, real forgiveness, and real progress. . . . It remains for us . . . to claim the blessings of the great Atonement." ("Testifying of the Great and Glorious Atonement," *Ensign*, Oct. 2001, 10, 15.)

That's the crux of it, isn't it? Do we claim the blessings of this atoning fire?

"And he cometh into the world that he may save all men if they will hearken unto his voice; for behold, he suffereth the pains of all men, yea, the pains of every living creature, both men, women, and children, who belong to the family of Adam.

"And he suffereth this that the resurrection might pass upon all men, that all might stand before him at the great and judgment day.

"And he commandeth all men that they must repent, and be baptized in his name, having perfect faith in the Holy One of Israel, or they cannot be saved in the kingdom of God." (2 Ne. 9:21–23.)

We must access the Atonement! We must figure out how to draw nearer to that warmth. Elder Neal A. Maxwell explained, "Since not all human sorrow and pain is connected to sin, the full intensiveness of the Atonement involved bearing our pains, infirmities, and sicknesses, as well as our sins. Whatever our sufferings, we can safely cast our 'care upon him; for he careth for [us]' (1 Peter 5:7)." (*Not My Will, But Thine* [Salt Lake City: Bookcraft, 1988], 51.)

Elder Bruce C. Hafen wrote, "Some Church members feel weighed down with discouragement about the circumstances of their personal lives, even when they are making sustained and admirable efforts. Frequently, these feelings of self-disappointment come not from wrongdoing, but from stresses and troubles for which we may not be fully to blame. The Atonement of Jesus Christ applies to these experiences because it applies to all of life. The Savior can wipe away all of our tears, after all we can do. . . .

"The Savior's atonement is . . . the healing power not only for sin, but also for carelessness, inadequacy, and all mortal bitterness. The Atonement is not just for sinners." ("Beauty for Ashes: The Atonement of Jesus Christ," *Ensign*, Apr. 1990, 7.)

If I want to partake of the warmth of this fire, I must repent often. I must keep my baptismal covenants. I must shed my layers of worldliness and allow my Heavenly Father's warmth to penetrate my will until my will becomes His will. I must allow Him to comfort me, even when I *want* to be sad, and allow Him to heal me even when I'm comfortable with my hurts and have grown used to them. I must allow Him to soften my very nature, to subdue my sarcasm, and help me let go of troubles.

Sister Anne C. Pingree, second counselor in the Relief Society general presidency, said, "It is essential to have Christ at the core of our lives. In these 'perilous times,' oh, how we need Him! He is the source of strength and safety. He is light. He is life. His peace 'passeth all understanding.' As our personal Savior and Redeemer, He invites us, one by one, with outstretched arms to 'come unto him.' . . . I testify that He is always there, His merciful, loving arms outstretched." ("Choose Ye Therefore Christ the Lord," *Ensign*, Nov. 2003, 110, 112.)

Sisters, come in from the cold. Warm yourselves by the fire of the Atonement. I testify that those loving, outstretched arms can warm your soul and chase away even the deepest, most aching cold.

Nephi's Psalm

I had a washing machine that occasionally got stuck on the rinse cycle. As wonderful as the rinse cycle is, it doesn't really facilitate the laundry getting done if it doesn't move through the agitation cycle and the spin cycle. If I didn't catch the rinse cycle when it got stuck, it just poured out water nonstop, filling up my drain field—usually when company came to visit.

That's why I often read Nephi's Psalm (see 2 Nephi 4). He had a faulty washer too. Nephi's Psalm helps me get my life out of the rinse cycle—the place where I just keep repeating and rehashing the same silly things instead of moving forward. To appreciate what I mean, let's break down Nephi's Psalm together.

First of all, Nephi gets stuck in the rinse cycle. He is disheartened by the death of his father, by the persecution he has received at the hands of Laman and Lemuel, and by his own perceived weaknesses:

"O wretched man that I am! Yea, my heart sorroweth because of my flesh; my soul grieveth because of mine iniquities.

"I am encompassed about, because of the temptations and the sins which do so easily beset me.

"And when I desire to rejoice, my heart groaneth because of my sins." (2 Ne. 4:17–19.)

As he pulls out of the cycle of discouragement, Nephi begins to count his blessings and acknowledge the help he has previously received from the Lord:

". . . nevertheless, I know in whom I have trusted.

"My God hath been my support; he hath led me through mine afflictions in the wilderness; and he hath preserved me upon the waters of the great deep.

"He hath filled me with his love, even unto the consuming of my flesh.

"He hath confounded mine enemies, unto the causing of them to quake before me.

"Behold, he hath heard my cry by day, and he hath given me knowledge by visions in the nighttime.

"And by day have I waxed bold in mighty prayer before him; yea, my voice have I sent up on high; and angels came down and ministered unto me.

"And upon the wings of his Spirit hath my body been carried away upon exceedingly high mountains. And mine eyes have beheld great things, yea, even too great for man; therefore I was bidden that I should not write them.

"O then, if I have seen so great things, if the Lord in his condescension unto the children of men hath visited men in so much mercy, why should my heart weep and my soul linger in the valley of sorrow, and my flesh waste away, and my strength slacken, because of mine afflictions?

"And why should I yield to sin, because of my flesh? Yea, why should I give way to temptations, that the evil one have place in my heart to destroy my peace and afflict my soul? Why am I angry because of mine enemy?" (2 Ne. 4:19–27.)

Nephi then begins to take heart. He remembers that the Lord has often supported him and has made covenants and promises with him to sustain him in the future if he is faithful. He turns a corner here, and decides to stand firm in the faith:

"Awake, my soul! No longer droop in sin. Rejoice, O my heart, and give place no more for the enemy of my soul.

"Do not anger again because of mine enemies. Do not slacken my strength because of mine afflictions." (2 Ne. 4:28–29.)

Nephi then prays for the strength to proceed. He covenants to follow and submit to the will of the Lord:

"Rejoice, O my heart, and cry unto the Lord, and say: O Lord, I will praise thee forever; yea, my soul will rejoice in thee, my God, and the rock of my salvation.

"O Lord, wilt thou redeem my soul? Wilt thou deliver me out of the hands of mine enemies? Wilt thou make me that I may shake at the appearance of sin?

"May the gates of hell be shut continually before me, because that my heart is broken and my spirit is contrite! O Lord, wilt thou not shut the gates of thy righteousness before me, that I may walk in the path of the low valley, that I may be strict in the plain road!

"O Lord, wilt thou encircle me around in the robe of thy righteousness! O Lord, wilt thou make a way for mine escape before mine enemies! Wilt thou make my path straight before me! Wilt thou not place a stumbling block in my way—but that thou wouldst clear my way before me, and hedge not up my way, but the ways of mine enemy." (2 Ne. 4:30–33.)

Finally, Nephi recommits his energies and turns from discouragement to hope and greater faith. He declares his trust in the Lord:

"O Lord, I have trusted in thee, and I will trust in thee forever. I will not put my trust in the arm of flesh; for I know that cursed is he that putteth his trust in the arm of flesh. Yea, cursed is he that putteth his trust in man or maketh flesh his arm.

"Yea, I know that God will give liberally to him that asketh. Yea, my God will give me, if I ask not amiss; therefore

I will lift up my voice unto thee; yea, I will cry unto thee, my God, the rock of my righteousness. Behold, my voice shall forever ascend up unto thee, my rock and mine everlasting God. Amen." (2 Ne. 4:34–35.)

That beautiful psalm was written by Nephi, and it belongs to him. But by using those same principles, we, as sisters in the gospel, can write our own psalms. Here's one from a single woman in her late forties:

"O silly woman that I am! Yea, I keep doing stupid things like filling out forms like these when I should be working. I'm surrounded by temptations like eating chocolates and drinking Mountain Dew. And I'm sorry that I don't seem to be stronger, that I sometimes give in. And when I desire to rejoice and attend movies at the theater and eat out at fancy restaurants, behold, I am usually sick of buttered popcorn and bloated with overeating because of my iniquities and inadequacies.

"However, there have been times when I prayed and received strength and support from my God. I remember receiving help from my Heavenly Father one time when I lost my car keys. He has also blessed me with a beautiful daughter, a wonderful job, and a nice home. He loves me enough that He forgives my short prayers, and tries to be patient with my whining, and blesses me with great friends.

"He blesses me so much that I shouldn't get frustrated with something so silly as my WEIGHT. And I shouldn't get mad at the mailman when he forgets to pick up my letters that are RIGHT IN FRONT OF HIS FACE, and I should have more patience with poor drivers.

"Awake, my soul! No longer droop in sin. Rejoice, O my heart. I WILL NOT GIVE UP TRYING! I will not GET DOWN ON MYSELF because I feel guilty. I will not give up my righteous goals of reading the Book of Mormon, even though I didn't make the deadline, and of trying to pray morning and night even when I'm too tired or late for work, and of trying not to swear (even when it seems so appropriate). I will not give up trying to be obedient just because I've made mistakes in the past. If the Lord helped me before, then I trust that He will help me now! I will lift up my voice unto my God in prayer because I know He answers prayers. I will pray for more faith, and more humility, and a worthy husband for my daughter. And I will never quit praying for help. Amen."

Here's another from a college student:

"O silly teenager that I am! [Yes, she picked the same adjective as the forty-year-old!] Yea, I keep doing stupid things like talking to myself when no one is looking. I'm surrounded by temptations, like drinking Coke. And I'm sorry that I don't seem to be stronger, that I sometimes give in. And when I desire to rejoice and attend football games and homecoming activities, and drive on cruise, behold, I am usually inundated by homework that I procrastinated.

"However, there have been times when I prayed and received strength and support from my God. I remember receiving help from my Heavenly Father one time when no one else could answer my questions. He has also blessed me with my family, my country, and my testimony. He loves me enough that He guides me, comforts me, and sent His Son to die for me. He blesses me so much that I shouldn't get frustrated with school and I shouldn't get mad at my family, and I should have more patience with my brother.

"Awake, my soul! No longer droop in sin. Rejoice, O my heart. I WILL NOT GIVE UP TRYING! I will not start skipping my meetings because I feel guilty or tired. I will not give up my righteous goals of a mission and temple marriage, of worthiness and purity. I will not give up trying to be obedient just because I've made mistakes in the past. If the Lord helped me before, then I trust that He will help me now! I will lift up my voice unto my God in prayer because I know He answers prayers. I will pray for guidance and answers and blessings. And I will never quit praying for help. Amen."

Here's another from a woman whose life is usually in crisis mode:

"O incredible over-scheduler that I am! Yea, I keep doing stupid things like trying to be everything for everyone and then getting mad when I can't achieve that goal. I'm surrounded by temptations like thinking, 'Gee, that looks fun. Why don't I try that?' and the temptation to quit everything altogether. And I'm sorry that I don't seem to be stronger, that I sometimes give in. And when I desire to rejoice and clean up the projects I've already started and slow the pace of life with riding horses again and swimming again, behold, I am usually too tired, too lazy, too preoccupied, too busy enabling others, and way too overscheduled (is no one listening?).

"However, there have been times when I prayed and received strength and support from my God. I remember receiving help from my Heavenly Father one time when I could not find the time to take Mom to her doctor appointments. He has also blessed me with a husband who tries to protect me from myself, people who are patient with me, and extended deadlines. He loves me enough that He forgives my occasional lack of preparation, my cries of frustration, and my tendency for sarcasm, and blesses me with opportunities to progress instead of just opportunities to be busy.

"He blesses me so much that I shouldn't get frustrated with something so silly as not being able to find the right hair length and style, shopping for groceries, and trying to find stamps for my letters. And I shouldn't get mad because people have learned to ignore my little fits, and I should have more patience with my mother who forgets to take her medicine, my daughter who refuses to pick up the clothes on the bedroom floor, and my son who dumps his hunting gear right by the door.

"Awake, my soul! No longer droop in sin. Rejoice, O my heart. I WILL NOT GIVE UP TRYING! I will not over-extend my energy just because I feel guilty or out of a sense of pure duty. I will not give up my righteous goals of over-coming negativity and pride and trying to build a savings account and trying not to lecture and moralize every time I write the kids a letter. I will not give up trying to be obedient just because I've made mistakes in the past. If the Lord helped me before, then I trust that He will help me now! I will lift up my voice unto my God in prayer because I know He answers prayers. I will pray for more faith, and more sensitivity to the Spirit, and to be softer and kinder and less self-involved. And I will never quit praying for help. Amen."

And here's one from an elderly woman's perspective:

"O forgetful old fool that I am! Yea, I keep doing stupid things like paying some bills twice and forgetting to pay the paper boy at all. I'm surrounded by temptations like sitting in the chair with a hot pad on my shoulders, watching TV, and postponing my visiting teachers yet again. And I'm sorry that I don't seem to be stronger, that I sometimes give in. And when I desire to rejoice and attend a fireside or have family home evening with my grandchildren, behold, I am usually too tired to get out of the chair and can usually talk myself out of it because of my iniquities and inadequacies.

"However, there have been times when I prayed and received strength and support from my God. I remember receiving help from my Heavenly Father one time when I forgot my son's birthday but managed to make him a cake and deliver it anyway. He has also blessed me with a warm home, a granddaughter that calls me every now and then, and a beautiful rose bush by my back door. He loves me enough that He forgives my half-hearted fasts; He sends a kind home teacher to change my light bulbs and still gives me a calling in the ward library so I'll be needed on Sundays.

"He blesses me so much that I shouldn't get frustrated with something so silly as my hearing aid. I shouldn't get mad at the grocery clerk who is impatient because I can't write out the check fast enough, and I should have more patience with long afternoons of waiting in doctors' offices.

"Awake, my soul! No longer droop in sin. Rejoice, O my heart. I WILL NOT GIVE UP TRYING! I will not let impatient people and advancing age get the best of me. I will not give up my righteous goals of reading the Relief Society lesson even though no one calls on me, and of trying to pray morning and night even when it's hard to get up off my knees, and trying not to tell my children how to raise my grandchildren. I will not give up trying to be obedient just because I've made mistakes in the past. If the Lord helped me before, then I trust that He will help me now! I will lift up my voice unto my God in prayer because I know He answers prayers. I will pray for more faith, more strength of character, better eyesight, and more stamina. And I will never quit praying for help. Amen."

I think everyone gets stuck in the rinse cycle now and then—you, me, Nephi, old women, young women, confident women, insecure women, women with bunions and corns, women in jeans, women in suits, single women, married women, women who were mothers to prophets, women who were married to prophets. We all have opportunities to become familiar with the rinse cycle. Elijah got stuck in the rinse cycle when he prayed to find a way to reach the children of Israel. Joseph Smith knew the rinse cycle well, as is evident by his prayer proffered from Liberty Jail. As we read the New Testament, we find that Martha apparently lived the rinse cycle in her kitchen.

It's no sin to be in the rinse cycle. It's only detrimental if we stay there too long. So the next time your washing machine gets stuck on the rinse cycle, tell your guests to go home and then call the repairman. If your life gets stuck in the rinse cycle, kick it into gear by applying Nephi's Psalm. Otherwise, you'll just get pruny fingers.

Tithing Chickens

When I was young, I didn't appreciate chickens much. I had to enter the henhouse with great care because we usually had a rooster who attacked me when I tried to gather eggs. I soon learned that to gather the eggs I had to carry something I could swing at the roosters as I made my way to the laying boxes. And then I had to watch my back as I gathered eggs in one hand and held the egg bucket in the other. The rooster wasn't the only treacherous thing in the henhouse—I had to wear boots because the faucet leaked, and the mixture of straw, manure, and feed that built up on the floor was thick and sticky.

Apparently I took my childhood knowledge of successful egg-gathering for granted until one day I sent six-year-old Homer out to gather the eggs. Suddenly I heard screams coming from the barnyard. I had no idea what was wrong—or even who was making the ruckus—until I got near the henhouse. Homer stood outside the henhouse door, pinning it shut behind him. He was crying as loudly as a mule brays, and he had a bloody nose. But he wasn't about to stop leaning against the henhouse door, because behind that door was a rooster who had decided to show a six-year-old who owned the farm.

As the story unfolded between sobs, I learned that the rooster had flown at Homer and, probably because of his short stature, had landed on his face. Homer was startled, so he yelled. That incited the rooster even more, and it flew at

Homer again. Homer swung the bucket at the rooster, breaking every single egg in the bucket, then ran to the door with the rooster in hot pursuit. Homer beat the rooster to the door, ran outside, and slammed the door shut, pinning the clawed terror inside the henhouse. I couldn't decide if Homer was still holding the door shut because he was frightened or because he was angry. I remember him wanting me to go get his dad and his dad's .22.

I managed to calm Homer down that day, but he never did like chickens—ever. Didn't like the smell, didn't like the eggs, didn't like anything about them. Years later I'd send him out to dump the kitchen scraps in their pen, and pretty soon I'd hear them squawking and flapping. I'd arrive to find Homer throwing the scraps at them, using the chickens for target practice. Everyone else gathered a dozen or more eggs at a time, but Homer only brought about five or six because he'd use the rest of the eggs to nail some poor unsuspecting chicken to the henhouse wall. If I sent Homer out to water the chickens, he sprayed them with the hose until they were running in circles. He had absolutely no respect for them at all.

Sometimes we learn lessons through strange means—and one winter I learned a valuable lesson through chickens. My husband and I had been farming for about twelve years when we found a farm that we thought we might be able to afford. We had acquired a few pieces of equipment, and we had a lot of heart and the ability to work hard. So we decided to stop farming for others and buy a farm for ourselves.

We ran into complications and couldn't sign the papers on the farm until late in the spring. The plowing and planting that should have been done the previous fall had not been done. Our ability to get all the spring plowing and planting done in time to grow a crop was critical to our ability to make our first payment. It was too late in the year for planting some kinds of crops, so we planted what we could. We ended up planting a lot of beans, because they can be planted late. By the time the irrigation season started, we were still trying to get the beans in.

That summer we worked harder than we ever had because we weren't familiar with the lay of the land, which feed ditches were necessary and which needed cleaning out, and which fields did and didn't irrigate well. It was a long, hot summer, and we spent most of it at the end of a shovel trying to get the crops to grow. The bean crop looked fair—a little scanty in spots, but passable. We were optimistic. We thought we might have a good year after all.

Then the frost came. It was earlier that year than it had been in many years, and it was a hard frost that destroyed most of the top leaves of our beans. The next night a second hard frost devastated the entire bean crop. Our dream was obliterated.

We had no idea what to do. Neighbors drove by to express their condolences. We went into survival mode, I guess—we just forged ahead and gathered what crops we could, not knowing what this would ultimately mean. We did have a hay field, and we cut the last crop of hay. As it lay in the fields to dry before it could be baled, a heavy rainstorm hit. It rained for days. The hay crop turned black.

I remember the Sunday it rained. Fred looked out the doors of the meetinghouse and with as hopeless a look as I had ever seen in his eyes said simply, "I'm going home." I suspect he cried.

We still had no idea what to do. Fred had farmed all our married life. We owed more money than we could ever pay back without a crop to harvest, and the bank cut off our operating loan. We had no income of any kind, only bills—bills for fertilizer, fuel, and seed. A farm payment would be due in four months, and we had nothing to pay it with—and no equity against which to borrow.

With no other options, we had to sell the equipment.

That was the easy part. We borrowed from family to help satisfy some debts. Fred took a part-time job feeding the neighbor's cows through the winter. His small paycheck brought in enough cash to pay for monthly fuel if we didn't go to town very often. It also paid the electricity and phone bill every month, but that was about all. There just wasn't any extra money that winter. But we had always paid our tithing before the financial disaster, and we continued to pay it, no matter how small our income was.

I was very grateful that winter to have potatoes in the cellar, a freezer full of meat, a basement full of canned fruits and vegetables, and a milk cow that produced. Still, I remember wishing we had money for little things, like fresh lettuce, cheese, or our weekly box of Sunday-morning cereal. I no longer wrapped foil around the baked potatoes, greased the tops of the bread loaves when they came out of the oven, or put sugar in the pancake batter. I figured out a dozen other little shortcuts that seemed to make our supplies stretch just a little further.

But we were fortunate—we didn't miss many essentials, except eggs. I dearly missed eggs. I found a few recipes that didn't use eggs, and that helped. And occasionally a twenty-dollar insurance reimbursement check came in, which allowed me to buy a dozen or two eggs now and then. Even then I was very frugal with them, not knowing when we could buy more.

The dark winter finally passed and Fred prepared his resume so he could find a job when spring came. We knew somehow we would make it through.

There were a few things that concerned me that spring, and I took them up with the Lord. It was time to plant a garden. I needed garden seeds, but I simply did not have the money for them. Our food storage had been severely depleted during the winter, and I knew I would need some garden produce to restock it. I needed garden seeds.

Another concern was that the insurance reimbursement checks had quit coming, so that bit of surprise income was gone. It's true: the kids had been healthier that winter than any other, and I was grateful that we had made no emergency trips to the doctor. Nonetheless, there was no bonus check in the mail to buy little things like eggs.

There was one more thing—if Fred found a job in town, he would need a new wardrobe. I seriously doubted he would find a job to which he could wear worn-out jeans and cowboy boots peppered with holes. But there was no cash for a new wardrobe.

Still, we paid tithing on any little income that came our way.

I had been discussing these matters with the Lord for a few weeks when my answers began to come. One day a neighbor lady called. Some months earlier she had purchased some laying chicks. They had grown and were producing, but my neighbor was tired of her "little project." She wanted someone to take the hens off her hands. Could I use them? I remember telling her "yes" immediately, even though I had no idea how I was going to feed them. I knew chicken mash was expensive.

A day or two later another neighbor called. He had some grain silos that needed cleaning out. Would Fred and the boys like to come and clean them out and keep the grain? Suddenly, I had chicken feed.

My next-door neighbor called that spring. As a grower for a local company, she and her husband had been given a box of garden seeds as a grower's gift. She had decided not to plant a garden that year. Could I use them? I was thrilled. I had very poor soil in my garden, but I had to try. Then another neighbor drove by. He needed shelter for his fertilizer trailer in case it rained and asked if he could park it in our shed. Of course I told him he could. He offered to give me a bucket of fertilizer for our garden in return for letting him park his trailer there. I assured him that was unnecessary, but I gratefully accepted the bucket of fertilizer.

Shortly after that, Grandma Erma wrote me a letter and tucked a hundred dollars in it. She said she remembered well the year Grandpa George had quit the farm and gone to town for work. She remembered how he needed to wear dress slacks and nice shirts and ties, and he was in need of a "town job" wardrobe. She sent the hundred dollars to help Fred buy a few things he might need for his new job.

These were only the most obvious answers to our prayers. In a hundred ways we had little blessings come. Now it's true that fifteen years later we're still making payments for farm debts we incurred that summer, and we probably will be for at least the *next* fifteen years. Still, I don't consider buying the farm a mistake. It was just one of those things that don't turn out despite our best efforts. And in spite of it all, I will still be grateful for those tithing chickens, and the tithing grain, and the tithing wardrobe money, and the tithing fertilizer, and the tithing garden seeds, and the hundred other little blessings that came to our family because we faithfully paid our tithing.

Five Loaves and Two Fishes

I am not a party thrower, which is okay—because I'm not really a *partygoer,* either. Nonetheless, there are times when I wish I was a better hostess. My twenty-fifth wedding anniversary came and went without celebration. My husband's fiftieth birthday will come soon, and it will also pass with no party. I did let the kids have birthday parties when they were eight and twelve—but invite a bunch of eight- and twelve-year-olds to a house, add chips, and it is a party.

There are a myriad of reasons for my reluctance to entertain, all of them lame. Here's one: I have sisters who are wonderful hostesses. Their homes are spotless, their towels match, they are good conversationalists, their food is great. They *are* a party. My home is never spotless, the only thing about my towels that match are the identical bleach stains, I stink at conversation, and I honestly think a baked potato, butter, and sour cream should cover any meal. The best tea party I ever threw was when I was seven: I served saltine crackers, chocolate chips, and chocolate milk. I remember this because it was the day my mother fixed boiled cow tongue for lunch. Unforgettable, right? Thank goodness for saltine crackers and chocolate.

Early in my marriage, I tried to help prepare food at my mother-in-law's house, but first I sliced the cucumbers wrong. (I had no idea there was more than one way to slice cucumbers.)

My mother-in-law then asked me to set the table, and I forged ahead without a tablecloth—major faux pas at her house. Although I got the knife on the correct side of the plate, I turned the blade the wrong way. She patiently pointed out my errors and tried to teach me a little refinement, and for years I tried to do better. I even bought a tablecloth to use whenever she came to visit at *my* home, but eventually I just gave up. Is it that important to use a tablecloth on a table I bought at a yard sale that is missing half the finish? If the purpose of a tablecloth (as it was explained to me) is to protect the table, then I just couldn't see the point. My table needed hiding, maybe, but not protecting.

I know my rationale is basically irrational. I know that just because my parties aren't perfect, I shouldn't quit trying to entertain. But you would just have to be inside my head to appreciate how traumatic the whole ordeal is for me. In fact, you don't have the time (or the interest, I'd wager) to hear about all my insecurities. I just have too many insecurities for one individual to maintain. It's a full-time job. So trust me, the advice you are about to receive comes from a pro.

Let me share the fable of an elderly Chinese woman who had two large pots; each hung on one end of a pole that she carried across her neck. One of the pots leaked because it had a crack in it, while the other pot was perfect and always delivered a full portion of water. At the end of the long walk from the stream to the house, the cracked pot arrived only half full. For two years this went on every day, with the woman bringing home only one and a half pots of water.

Of course, the perfect pot was proud of its accomplishments, but the poor cracked pot was ashamed of its imperfection and miserable that it could do only half of what it had been made to do. After two years of what it perceived to be bitter failure, it spoke to the woman one day by the stream.

"I am ashamed of myself, because this crack in my side causes water to leak out all the way back to your house," it cried.

The old woman smiled. "Did you notice that there are flowers on your side of the path, but not on the other pot's side? That's because I have always known about your flaw, so I planted flower seeds on your side of the path. Every day as we walk back to the house, you water them. For two years I have picked these beautiful flowers to decorate my table. Without you being just the way you are, there would not be this beauty to grace my house."

The truth is, each of us feels somewhat like the cracked pot. In one way or another, we each feel somewhat inadequate. But if we're really honest with ourselves, we will also admit that we have done some things not so badly; perhaps there are even some things we do quite well. We just hate admitting it because, after all, we wouldn't want to be caught bragging. It's also a fact that no matter how well you do something, someone somewhere will be able to do it better, which means failure is just around the next corner—and that's a crack that's hard to overlook. But what a shame.

I propose that cracked pots are not only inevitable, they're essential. Through our shortcomings, the glory of God can be manifest if we invite Him to participate, to magnify us.

"And if men come unto me I will show unto them their weakness. I give unto men weakness that they may be humble; and my grace is sufficient for all men that humble themselves before me; for if they humble themselves before me, and have faith in me, then will I make weak things become strong unto them." (Ether 12:27.)

In other words, a weak moment can be turned into a sacred moment of worship if we invite and allow the Lord to use His power to enlarge our effort. Look at how He can enlarge even the most meager efforts:

"When Jesus then lifted up his eyes, and saw a great company come unto him, he saith unto Philip, Whence shall we buy bread, that these may eat?

"And this he said to prove him: for he himself knew what he would do." (John 6:5–6.)

Philip answered, telling Jesus that there was not enough money to buy bread for all the people. Then Andrew, another disciple, said, "There is a lad here, which hath five barley loaves and two small fishes." (John 6:9.)

"And when he had taken the five loaves and the two fishes, he looked up to heaven, and blessed, and brake the loaves, and gave them to his disciples to set before them; and the two fishes divided he among them all.

"And they did all eat, and were filled.

"And they took up twelve baskets full of the fragments, and of the fishes.

"And they that did eat of the loaves were about five thousand men." (Mark 6:41–44.)

I cannot throw a party, but I can do math—and one little boy plus five loaves plus two fishes plus Christ equals enough and to spare. It's interesting to me that there are three specific parts to this particular event: there were barley loaves, there were fish, and there was the power of Jesus Christ. With all my insecurities, I cannot throw a party. However, I can make a potato salad. I can wash windows. I can turn the barbequing, tables, and chairs over to Fred, and I can invite Christ to help me make the most of it. Ergo, party.

Now, don't laugh as you wonder whether Christ will care about my party. I think He will care about my party if it is an opportunity to associate with good people, to strengthen relationships, to fellowship and be fellowshipped. Yes, I think He will care. He will also care about helping me develop a social skill. As a matter of record, to anyone who takes what talents they have (even if it's only potato salad and window washing) and makes the most of them, the Lord says, "Well done, good and faithful servant; thou hast been faithful over a few things, I will make thee ruler over many things: enter . . . into the joy of thy lord." (Matt. 25:23.)

Douglas M. Chabries discusses this very thing (see "Talents," *Brigham Young University Speeches,* 17 May 2005) and suggests elements that will aid the process of developing talents. Prayer should always be involved, inviting Christ into the equation. Another essential element is listening and receiving the impressions that come as a result of that prayer. Choosing good friends who can lift us, believe in us, teach us, and inspire us to be better will assist our efforts.

Obedience is always a key to progression. Obedience frees us up to recognize and accept opportunities. Disobedience creates complications.

Remembering who we are as spirit daughters of our Heavenly Father can give us the confidence that seeds of divine talent lie within us, just waiting for water. Perhaps we will stumble across them as we accept callings. Perhaps we will uncover them as trials overcome us. Pay attention to compliments—be humble if you must, but pay attention. What may seem ordinary to you is not so ordinary for someone else, and is likely a gift you possess. Develop the gift.

Finally, seek refinement. Find something that you think is beautiful, trim your sails, and go out and meet it. It may mean taking some lessons. It may mean checking a book out of a library. It may mean attending a class. Don't think you can do that? Just remember: a boat that is harbored at the dock will likely not catch the fish.

President Gordon B. Hinckley has said, "I . . . invite [you] to rise to the great potential within you. I do not ask that you reach beyond your capacity. I hope you will not nag your-selves with thoughts of failure. I hope you will not try to set goals far beyond your capacity to achieve. I hope you will simply do what you can do in the best way you know. If you do so, you will witness miracles come to pass." ("Motherhood: A Heritage of Faith," [Salt Lake City: Deseret Book, 1995], 9.)

Every time I throw a tablecloth on the table for company, I count on those miracles. Every time I sit down to sew a quilt, I count on those miracles. Every time I stand at a pulpit or try to write a story for the grandkids, I count on those miracles. Every time my boss comes to me with a project that I have not attempted before, I count on those miracles. I have plenty of little loaves and fishes, and I trust that God has plenty of miracles—even enough and to spare.

Abundant Lives

First of all, it wasn't my fault the finch died. Here's the thing—Mom left the bird for me to take care of. It lived fewer than twenty-four hours. That's not even long enough to starve to death or chill to death or anything to death. There's no way I can be blamed for that one. His time was just up.

And you can't pin the second finch's death on me, either. Here's the thing—Mom didn't feed it. She thought she did. She changed the paper in the cage, she refilled the water, she put gravel in there for its gullet. She just forgot the feed. This created a very stiff bird. Again, not my fault. I just happened to be the one who found it.

The frog's death could perhaps be pinned on me if I had only an average defense lawyer. But here's the thing—no one can really prove I killed it because we haven't found the body. No body, no crime. It was such a cute little thing, only about as big as a thumbnail. I thought my grandson would like to see it, so I put it in a tall spaghetti noodle jar. That night, I thought I'd better crack the lid just a teensy bit so it could get air. I propped the lid open about one-sixteenth of an inch. The next morning the lid was still propped but the jar was empty. The only place I haven't looked is under the fridge and in the heating vents. But, as I said, no body, no crime. Can't prove a thing. I *did* find a frog on the floor of my shower about four months later, although I cannot technically prove it was the same one. If it was the same frog, I cannot even begin to fathom what it had been doing for four months.

I am definitely guilty of killing the mice. I even enjoyed the conquest. But here's the thing—there's a stray tomcat that eats the evidence when I throw the mangled little bodies over the fence into the pasture. Again, no body, no crime. Only my admission could convict me, but I could plead duress. I could even plead self-defense. Besides, who cares about mice, anyway? Nobody but Cinderella—and she got a castle, so she doesn't count.

There *was* that one kitten, but here's the thing—it shouldn't have lived anyway. It was sickly and had been deserted by its mother. The cat's mother is to blame. It's true that I didn't nurse it back to health, but there's really no proof that I could have saved it anyway. I'd be acquitted for lack of evidence.

The only reason I mention this in the first place is because I was wondering how many little bits of nothing it takes to add up to something. It's probably a mathematical improbability. Yet something tells me that even though some things are incredibly insignificant, if we add a bunch of them up, they may equal something significant.

A newspaper column explained something of this phenomenon. "Shooting stars, falling stars, meteors—different names for the same thing: tiny bits of space debris plunging into the atmosphere at literally blazing speeds . . . Each is typically about the size of a grain of sand.

"So it begs the question: Is Earth getting heavier, and if so, what are the consequences?

"Not counting the relatively rare meteors large enough to survive all the way to the ground it's estimated that meteors dump about 120 tons of material onto the Earth every day (plus or minus 60 tons or so). Isaac Newton's famous law of gravity tells us that the gravitational force between Earth and the sun . . . is proportional to Earth's mass. So as Earth gets heavier, it should feel a stronger pull toward the sun, causing us to spiral in.

"To put this 'danger' in perspective, consider that Earth weighs about 600 quintillion tons (that's a six followed by 20 zeroes). Even a millennium's worth of meteoric bulking up would amount to less than one 100-billionth of a percent of the Earth's total mass. Total it over Earth's 4.5 billion-year age, and it still only adds up to four 100ths of 1 percent . . . In short, long before we face the danger of spiraling into the sun, other astronomical catastrophes will have befallen our world." (Chris Anderson, *Times-News*, 26 Mar. 2006.)

It would seem, then, that both assumptions are true—something insignificant can only be significant when compounded over a very long period of time. But over a long period of time it does amount to something significant.

Why do I care? Well, here's the thing—Elder Joseph B. Wirthlin suggested, ". . . those who live abundant lives . . . with the help of their Heavenly Father, create a masterpiece of their lives." ("The Abundant Life," *Ensign,* May 2006, 101.) I've been thinking about that. How would a masterpiece be created? One stroke at a time, I suppose. One stroke—relatively insignificant—when added to another insignificant stroke and then another could, over time, become relatively significant. In fact, it could become a masterpiece.

I wonder how many strokes artists use to create masterpieces. I wonder how many strokes Van Gogh's *Starry Night* took. How many strokes did it take to create *Whistler's Mother?* I don't know, but somehow I think these artistic masterpieces took only a very few strokes when compared with the strokes required to create a life's masterpiece. Each stroke, by itself, is insignificant—almost—very close to nothing. Yet in this case, bits of nothing added up to something. I guess the only thing that remains to be seen are the strokes of my life's masterpiece.

Mathematically speaking, if nothing plus nothing equals nothing, then the strokes of our lives must be *something*. Each stroke, though seemingly insignificant, counts. I can name several strokes that by themselves seem insignificant, almost nothing—like one trip to go visiting teaching, saying a single blessing on the food, teaching a lesson, studying a scripture. Maybe a priesthood holder wearing a white shirt on Sunday is a seemingly insignificant stroke. Maybe apologizing to someone who doesn't even accept the apology is a seemingly insignificant stroke. I've talked with people about the Church with no apparent effect. I've taught lessons to seminary students who slept through the whole thing (I don't blame them, really; sometimes I bore myself). Looking at each isolated little effort makes me go cross-eyed.

But here's the thing—each simple, seemingly insignificant stroke adds up to something. How significant is a drop of water? If a stalactite could talk, what would it say about the importance of a drop of water?

If my life is a painting, then how's my masterpiece coming? If I stand back and observe my life from a distance, how am I doing? If I'm not focusing on the brush stroke of one single apology or the brush stroke of one single lesson, but can look at my life in total, how's my masterpiece coming?

My daughter told me the other day, "Mom, you're pretty sane." I asked her what she meant. She said, "Well, considering some of the things you've been through, I think you're pretty sane." I didn't know whether to send her to her bedroom or thank her. I think she was trying to pay me a compliment, but it wasn't quite what I had in mind. How many people walking through an art gallery look at a masterful piece and say, "Yes, that is so sane"? Nobody. Instead, we say, "My, that's a beautifully balanced piece," or "This one has such grace and harmony and strong lines." But me? Nope, just sane. Nonetheless, sane is good, and certainly better than the alternative. I can work with sane. I can improve sane.

I think all great women built their lives one stroke at a time. A Marjorie Pay Hinckley did not just "happen" one day. A Ruth did not just wake up one day and find that she was noble. Sariah, Hannah, Esther—list them all. Their masterpieces, I believe, were created; they didn't just happen, and creation is a process. Creation, even for the Lord, is a process.

When I look into the heavens and see falling stars and realize that they are only grains of sand, I am reminded of the Lord's process of creation—each grain of sand is part of the masterpiece. Though students may sleep through my lessons, sisters may never answer their doorbells, and one little expression of gratitude over a meal may be hurried, the strokes will ultimately speak for themselves.

We'll go cross-eyed if we look at life's brushstrokes one at a time. While looking at the whole picture, though, I've learned that each little brushstroke is absolutely significant . . . and that I should never, ever be trusted with frogs, finches, or cats.

Merry-Go-Round Rides

We used to do some awfully dangerous things as kids. It was a different day, I suppose—a different time. As just one example, we had some grazing land about fifty miles from our home. When it was time to move cows, we loaded horses into our stock truck—I think it was as many as eight or ten horses, though I'm not exactly sure. The stock truck accommodated the horses nicely, but it was mathematically and physically impossible to get all of the riders in the cab of the same truck along with their coats, hats, boots, the lunch cooler, and whatever other gear was necessary for the trip.

The possibilities were narrowed even further by the fact that the driver (my dad) weighed more than two hundred pounds, and so did at least one other passenger. His name was Emmett, and he always smelled of wild onions and garlic—and he never failed to show the victim squished next to him the shrapnel in his arm from an old war wound, as if he hadn't shown it to you on the three dozen previous trips. To top it off, there was a gear shift on the floorboard that had to be maneuvered around the knees. For all these reasons, the cab may have been safe, but it was not big enough—and it was certainly not a popular place to be.

That's why my brothers and sisters and I perched on top of the truck cab with our backs to the horses, our legs dangling over the front windshield, hanging on to the cattle rack for dear life, our hair lashing our faces in the wind, rain, and sleet. It was always a white-knuckle trip for me. The space between the cab and the cattle rack looked wide enough for me to fall through if I fell asleep or failed to pay attention, and I could see the graveled road zipping past beneath us. There were plenty of flattened jackrabbits, polecats, kittens, and ground squirrels on our country roads, and I could clearly picture myself flattened beneath the cattle truck. I wondered how long it would take me to bloat and stink. With an imagination like that, it was always a dilemma whether to choose the bone-crunching cab or the death defying roof.

And tractor bucket rides—those were dangerous as well, but no one seemed too concerned about them at the time. Sometimes the adults even ran to get the camera. What were they thinking? These days there are safety buttons, latches, full-body harnesses, buckles, helmets, shin guards, elbow pads, and Plexiglas goggles. Back then it was, "Come on, you kids—if you dangle your legs over the front of the bucket we can get more in. Everybody smile!" "Higher, Dad, higher!"

And what about rides in the back of the pickup truck? Back there with the tires and shovels, barbed wire, salt blocks, wet dogs, siphon tubes, ditch dams, nails, steel posts, and post driver? All those dangerous metal objects, and not once did someone suggest a helmet. No one cared if kids hung over the side to grab tree branches. The only concern was that a hat didn't fly off in the process—your own hat, of course. Anyone else's didn't matter. Today people won't let an animal ride in the back of a pickup truck unless it's safely protected in a pet carrier, but in my day it was everybody for himself—and if you got hurt, someone usually said, "Well, I hope she's learned her lesson."

Even the school playground equipment was dangerous. Our teachers used to yell at us for climbing on the three-story metal fire escape, but I have news for them—the steep metal slide and the merry-go-round were three times the threat. The slide nicked our bare legs and ripped our dresses. The merry-go-round was more like an I-dare-you-go-round.

This merry-go-round was not a flat disc about eight inches off the ground on which kids sat in the center to keep from flying off. No, it was a tubular metal ride that bore many similarities to white-knuckle stock-truck rides. There was no disc, no platform. We sat with our bottoms hanging over the pipe at the perimeter, our feet dangling at least two feet off the ground and our hands gripping a second pipe as we watched the gravel whirl beneath us. The real thrill was to jump between the outer bars and push the wheel as fast as possible. It was thrilling because if our feet faltered or we couldn't keep the pace or we missed our aim when jumping onto the bar, we bit the dust—or the gravel and cinder in this case. It was death-defying. There are probably bits of gravel permanently embedded in the knees of every elementary student who ever attended that school.

I could never decide whether I liked the merry-go-round. The monkey bars (or should I say "blister bars"?) didn't compare—they only caused calluses and tendonitis. But the chances of actually being mangled were best on the merry-go-round. Parts of the ride were exciting, dizzying, and thrilling. Other parts made my stomach tumble and jump. And still other parts just scared me spitless.

I still believe it was outright dangerous, but it was the most popular piece of equipment on the playground, and I couldn't seem to leave it alone. Several times I went home with ripped clothing and bloody knees, and I'm not quite sure why I kept going back. Maybe I was addicted to the awful rush of excitement, or maybe I just wanted to conquer it—and the challenge kept bringing me back. Maybe it spun so fast that I just didn't know how to get off.

But that wasn't the only merry-go-round I rode, and it wasn't the only one I had trouble getting off. For years I rode a merry-go-round of unhappiness built on other people's choices. One poor choice by someone I cared about started the spin. That poor choice was followed by another poor choice, and the wheel spun faster and faster. Finally it spun so fast that I couldn't figure out how to get off. It was a miserable ride. It made me queasy and sick to my stomach. It gave me headaches. Still, I couldn't figure out how to get off—how to quit spinning and quit getting caught in the whirl.

I didn't figure it out for years. I prayed often enough, although I probably prayed for the wrong thing. Nonetheless, after many, many prayers, I woke up one morning with a hymn stuck in my head: "Know This, That Every Soul Is Free." I was pretty sure it was an answer to my prayers; I just couldn't figure out how. I ran through the words of the hymn in my mind and tried to apply them to my merry-go-round.

> Know this, that ev'ry soul is free
> To choose his life and what he'll be;
> For this eternal truth is giv'n
> That God will force no man to heav'n.
>
> He'll call, persuade, direct aright,
> And bless with wisdom, love, and light,
> In nameless ways be good and kind,
> But never force the human mind. (*Hymns*, 240.)

Well, who needed to hear that? The more I thought about it, the madder I got. This was my answer? I already knew that the person who was making poor choices was free to do so. *That* was the cause of my pain. I certainly didn't need to be reminded of it. However, the third consecutive day that the hymn was running through my head, I decided the Lord was trying to tell me something important—and I wasn't getting it.

Early that morning I had a few minutes of peace and quiet before a meeting. Conveniently enough, a hymn book was nearby. I turned to "Know This, That Every Soul Is Free" and went over the words again. Nothing. Then I saw the scriptures noted at the bottom of the hymn and decided to look them up. I read the words of Samuel the Lamanite to the Nephites:

"And now remember, remember, my brethren, that whosoever perisheth, perisheth unto himself; and whosoever doeth iniquity, doeth it unto himself; for behold, ye are free; ye are permitted to act for yourselves; for behold, God hath given unto you a knowledge and he hath made you free.

"He hath given unto you that ye might know good from evil, and he hath given unto you that ye might choose life or death; and ye can do good and be restored unto that which is good, or have that which is good restored unto you; or ye can do evil, and have that which is evil restored unto you." (Hel. 14:30–31.)

There it was—my answer. Yes, everyone is free to choose, including me. I am free to choose to get off the merry-go-round. I am free to let the merry-go-round spin without me. I can choose to be happy in spite of the choices of others. Moroni must have known this. Mormon must have known this. They experienced anguish due to the hard-hearted and stiffnecked people, but they didn't get on the merry-go-round. They didn't become hopeless and lose focus or lose footing. They were surely saddened, but nonetheless took heart in the comforting thought that they would soon see their God and find peace. They also had the assurance that their posterity would someday have access to gospel covenants. So regardless of the wickedness that swirled around them, they didn't ride the merry-go-round. That was my answer. Someone finally gave me permission to get off the merry-go-round.

So if you find your head spinning, if you find yourself unable to focus on happiness and the good things in life, then this is for you: Go ahead. Samuel the Lamanite and I give you permission to get off the merry-go-round.

Something Physical

Pretty Much Anything Works

Something physical is a very broad category. Pay attention.

One night Fred decided to teach me how to irrigate, largely because his back was hurting and he was stooped over and walking funny. He said it would save him a lot of bending. So I dressed for the part in red plaid pajama pants and flip-flops, and I tripped through the orchard after him. Only he didn't seem to think it was necessary to check the progress of the apricots and apples, as I did.

We got to the ditch and he showed me how to put the boards in the cement board-holder slot things. I'm pretty sure I could have figured this part out on my own. However, there were a couple of boards that didn't fit—and since our ditch system is twenty-five years old, I thought that was odd. Fred explained that he made new boards because he shredded the old ones with the lawnmower. Yup, that would explain it.

I tried to show him the little snail shells that were clumped up in a pile in the bottom of the ditch. He limped away unimpressed.

By the time we got to the last cement thingy, my pajama pants were wet at the knees and drooping, which made them longer, so I kept tripping on them. By this time something sticky between my foot and the flip-flops demanded my attention, which I gave it. That was a good thing, because I also noticed that I needed to paint my toenails, and a shade of peach might be nice. Fred did not seem to appreciate this latest observation any more than he did my observation of the snail shells. In response, he simply sent me for the shovel so he could set the dam.

I've set dams before and didn't feel I needed a refresher course, so after I fetched the shovel I went to uncoil and string out the hoses. Since I was so close to the house, I decided to go check on the potatoes that were boiling on the stove. I had to step carefully, of course, because Rachel had just mopped the kitchen floor, and I was afraid she'd catch me sneaking across it. At that point, of course, I stopped by Granny's bedroom to grab some chocolate. Finally, I decided I'd better go to the bathroom while I was in the house.

By the time I got back outside, Fred was nowhere to be found. At that point, I did the only responsible thing possible: I tried to find the missing nut that was causing the little sign thingy by the ditch to hang a little crooked. I couldn't find it, so I went to the shop to find a replacement nut and to get a screwdriver while I was waiting for Fred to be found. Have you ever tried to find something in a husband's shop? Yeah . . . that would be why he had already found himself and started the ditch pump before I got back.

I emerged from the shop with my little square nut and a screwdriver, but I didn't have any luck fixing the sign, so I asked Fred to try. He looked at me like I had just pointed out the snail shells again. He took a stab at it, though, and when he couldn't fix it he blamed the screwdriver. Of course he blamed the screwdriver. He's a man. He said our next job was to adjust the sprinklers. He went one direction, so I went the other.

I stood back about fifty feet or so from the nearest sprinkler and observed it going pish-pish-pish very, very quickly (want to hear it again? Pish-pish-pish . . .)—far too quickly for me to run in there and adjust it without getting my red pajamas all wet. I decided it looked just fine.

Now you know why I don't give you more details of our lives. That's four minutes of *your* life you'll never get back again. However, I can count the whole thing as my exercise for the day. It was a workout—bending, reaching, sneaking, screwing, searching, observing, and scooping snail shells.

A few nights later I accomplished another workout. Jenny, Rachel, and I went to four-year-old Austin's t-ball game. We carried lawn chairs, cameras, drinks, two little boys, hats, blankets, diaper bags, and a dump truck the length of a football field to the baseball diamond where a lot of little boys were running around in brand-new blue hats and knee-length blue shirts. They looked like a bunch of little blueberries.

Poor Austin. He had never been past first base before because he always hit the ball to the pitcher (the only one paying attention), who always threw it to the first baseman (the only one who can catch). But that night the first baseman missed the ball, so Austin's coach told him to run to second. It was difficult to see the base in the grassy baseball field, so Austin ran first towards right field and then into center field looking for it. The whole time he was completely unaware that another little blueberry was chasing him with a ball. Austin was tagged out, of course.

The whole concept of the game is a bit foreign to Austin, as it apparently is to the other eight little blueberries on his team. Throughout the game, the coach kept yelling, "Get up! Don't lie down." Soft grass with lots of spiders and things in it? How can a four-year-old not lie down in that? The coach had other instructions as well:

"Austin, quit climbing the backstop."

"Austin, don't forget your glove."

"Austin, your glove is on the wrong hand."

"Austin, quit playing in the dirt—and watch the ball."

"Austin, quit playing catch with your mitt."

"Austin, pay attention."

By then everybody knew Austin's name, if they didn't know it before.

Do you know how boring it is to be in the outfield during T-ball? It's like watching paint dry. But it's pretty entertaining to watch the outfielders be bored. At one point the coach had to sit in the outfield with them because the boys were playing tag.

I decided during the game that my sympathies are with Austin. Do we really care that he gets the concept of baseball at the age of four? I'm forty-seven, and I still think it's a dumb game. You know why it's the national pastime, don't you? Beer. Lots of beer. What else could make you like hotdogs? What else could numb your mind enough to convince you that what you're doing is worthwhile? Two-year-old Wyatt was the only one really having a good time. He ran around and pushed his dump truck and sipped on juice and went to the store for more pop with Rachel.

After the game, Austin's coach gave the team sippy juices and fruit leather, so Austin felt the game was a success. Then we carried lawn chairs, cameras, empty drinks, two little boys, hats, blankets, diaper bags, and a dump truck the length of a football field back to the car again. That's a lot of exercise.

But it didn't end there. As I drove home, I rolled down my windows. Do you know how many smells there are between the T-ball field and the city of Hansen? There's a dairy smell, the smell of summer barbeques through Kimberly, and the smell of wet alfalfa fields toward Twin Falls. I smelled the sugar factory. There's a gasoline smell when you drive by the 7-Eleven and South Park, the smell of freshly mown lawns toward the city of Filer, and the roadkill skunk smell just down the road from my house. I know these smells have nothing to do with exercise, but since they involve the nasal passages and olfactory senses, they fall into the category of "Something Physical." As I said, it's a broad category. That's my story, and I'm sticking to it.

Track

I had an illustrious high school track career—all two weeks of it. I don't know why I even tried out for track. I hated wind. I hated being cold. I hated being singled out. I hated running until I felt like puking. And do you know what wind, cold, being singled out, and puking add up to? Track.

I suppose I just wanted something to do. Instead, I got something to hate. It didn't help that my older sister Marcia was a track hero. She was a sprinter. She broke records. She won medals. I think another older sister, Lila, also ran track, although I'm a little fuzzy about it. At any rate, how many track genes are there to go around in one family? Probably two—and they were used up by my older sisters.

But you have to hear about my two-week track career. (Everybody else has.) It was painfully obvious that I was not fast. Do you know where they put the not-fast kids? In distance events. Do you have any idea how many times around the track distance events take? If you did, we wouldn't need to have this discussion. Since you don't, I'll tell you: they are longer than a phone call from your aunt when you really have to go to the bathroom. They are longer than high school graduation exercises on the backless top bleacher in a suffocating gymnasium. They are longer than the line at the post office during your twenty-minute lunch hour. They are longer than staff meetings.

And so I began my career in the 800-meter run (880-yard run in those days). That meant twice around the track. Twice. Because I had never run this particular race before (or any other), I complained to the coach.

"I don't even know how to run this race." (You know, like I had a repertoire of running styles and formats from which to choose.)

"All you have to do is keep up with Debbie," she said.

Well, that was just dandy. Debbie happened to be the fastest girl in southern Idaho. I'm not even sure why Debbie was competing in this race; she smoked the competition in the 100-meter run. Maybe they were just testing her range.

So Debbie and I went to the starting line. The gun went off, and away we went. I learned several things during that race. First, you don't jog in distance races. Who knew? We started at a dead run, forming a tight pack and jostling for the lead. I kept my eyes focused on two things: the track and Debbie's heels. That was my goal—never lose sight of Debbie's heels.

By the end of the first trip around the track we were still on a dead run and we were still in a tight pack. I was dying. And then it happened. As we were running on the inside edge of that tight pack, Debbie did something I was totally unprepared for. She ran off the track onto the infield. She limped like she had pulled a muscle or something. And I was right on her heels. We were out of the race.

I was never so grateful to Debbie as I was in that moment. I couldn't have kept up that pace for another lap. So there it was. I had quit. Pretty funny for someone who hated being singled out. I quit a race. No one quits a race. At least Debbie had the forethought to go out with a limp.

The reason you had to painfully relive this with me is because you need to know what the consequences have been. All these years later, while on my morning jog, I was thinking about quitting track. Yeah—forty-seven years old and jogging, and this by someone who quit track. But there's a reason I jog—walking takes too long. I tried power walking, but I daydream, and my power walking turns into a leisurely stroll. I tried a treadmill, but it's hard to hear the TV over the ruckus of the treadmill. I thought about joining a gym, but who wants to pay for the privilege of looking that bad in the company of others? I thought about taking a dancing class, but the whole leotard thing at forty-seven was just . . . ick. I thought about swimming, but swimming makes my freckles turn green. I know, I shouldn't care about all these vanities, but I'm forty-seven—I'm not dead.

So penance for quitting track has been a lifetime of jogging, aching muscles, gnats in my teeth, and then quitting. Then starting again, with more aching muscles, more gnats in my teeth, and then quitting again. It's a cycle that goes on for infinity. And it's still cold and it's still windy.

It bites. The only upside to the situation is that I'm approaching fifty, and at least I won't be living as long as Adam, who lived more than nine hundred years. Nine hundred years of track or jogging? That truly has to be the definition of perdition.

So when you pick something physical—and you're walking or kick boxing or enjoying aerobics, when you're trying to get your figure back after having a baby or turning forty, or when you're just jumping on the trampoline with the kids and wishing you'd gone to the bathroom first, or when you're running across the yard to get to the telephone, or when you're huffing and puffing up the stairs with another load of laundry, remember this: you don't have to succeed at being a fitness guru. I didn't necessarily have to succeed at the 800-meter race. Both of us, however, have to keep at it. As Dorie the fish wisely sings in *Finding Nemo,* "Just keep swimming, swimming, swimming. Just keep swimming."

Failing Forward

I found out something about myself last summer. I was flying through the air on a rope swing over a deep ravine, toes practically scraping the treetops, and miles and miles from the nearest ambulance. I found that I could not get my George of the Jungle tree-smashing yodel out of my throat because I had swallowed my tongue. I found that I needed to watch others (a lot of others—okay, okay . . . everyone) try it before I would risk it. After all, I am a grandma. I have birthday parties decorated with pipe-cleaner butterflies yet to attend. I have a grandchild's first loose tooth to celebrate.

I also found that it took three sons to hoist me onto the swing because I lacked confidence in my biceps. (Funny thing, though: when your life is on the line, you'd be surprised how well your biceps can come through for you.) I found that getting on the swing and zooming up over the pine trees was the easy part (once I was actually launched). Finally, I found that the troubling part was the dismount on the side of the steep ravine.

Stressful situations, whether in the form of a rope swing or otherwise, seem to bring out in us things we can never discover elsewhere. When stressful situations arise, we may find out we're more courageous than we thought—or maybe we discover we're more chicken. Maybe we thought we were smarter or more versatile. Maybe we found we were more biased, less articulate, more stubborn. Or maybe we weathered things rather well and were surprised at our ability to adapt. Whatever we learn, like it or not, stress is the catalyst for self-discovery.

There are entire seminars dealing only with stress—how to reduce it, how to manage it, how to avoid it. I've decided I don't really need a seminar or a therapist for self-discovery— what I need, occasionally, is a rope swing and a deep ravine. The kind of stress I got from the rope swing and the deep ravine lasted only a moment and was very self-revealing. You only have to feel your heart banging against your Adam's apple once every year or so to remember what's trivial in life (like not enough money to stop at a yard sale to pick up one more thing that you don't need and will throw out in a year, or the person driving in front of you who is talking on the cell phone . . . oh wait, that's me . . .) and what's important in life (like the ability to breathe and the ability to choose between right and wrong).

Part of my stress comes from the fact that men get to go through a midlife crisis and no one questions it. I decided I wanted one—a crisis. So I had one. I called several dance schools until I found one that had a tap dance class for adults. They didn't even care that I had no experience. They didn't care that I had no leotard. They didn't care that I'm clumsy as all-get-out. As long as my checkbook showed up, they simply didn't care. I think this is wisdom on their part as well as mine.

My boss recently asked about my plan for reducing stress, since I listed that as one of my goals for this year. You know how employers make you come up with goals. It's their attempt to make subordinates believe that they care. It just makes the cold, sterile bureaucracy feel so warm and fuzzy. It's almost enough to give my metal filing cabinet goose bumps.

Since I couldn't think of anything to put on my goal sheet for the year, I had listed stress reduction as a goal. I had not been successful. Not only had my stress increased, my job duties expanded, four adult children moved home, and my dog died, but now I faced the stress of reaching my stress-reducing goal. Whose genius idea was this?

That's why I took up tap dancing. It's more like thud-dancing. It's a lot like shuffle dancing. It's actually thud-shuffle dancing most of the time. I know, you're way ahead of me. It didn't reduce stress—it shifted it. For instance, I had to decide what outfit would allow me to clumsily thud-shuffle without revealing jiggles where jiggles were never intended to be. I could wear my striped pajama bottoms—the varnish stains should come out any washing now. I could wear jeans—if I could zip them. I could wear my bib overalls, but that would mean three extra pounds to hoist into each tap.

Then there's the stress of deciding whether I should exercise before I go to class. Actually, the class IS for exercise, but maybe I should exercise a lot beforehand so that I won't get out of breath, so that I won't jiggle, and so I will look more graceful. It's a little like wondering whether to clean the house before the maid arrives (I wouldn't want a maid to see the house dirty) or whether I should pre-mow the lawn before I hire the neighbor to come and mow it. Who would do that, right? Well—me. Maybe. It doesn't have to make sense. It's just built into the psyche. I didn't put it there.

Let's just pretend that I've solved the wardrobe issue and decided not to exercise before class (who was I kidding anyway?). With those stressful decisions out of the way, I can move straight to the bigger issue: I can never, ever tell anyone that I'm tap dancing. I'm almost fifty years old. That's a visual image I cannot impose on anyone. It could scar them for life. On the other hand, can I keep a secret? Yeah, like that's gonna happen.

I'm going to reduce my stress by creating stress. Good, huh? Can that be wise? What is wisdom, anyway? Solomon was said to have wisdom. But he had seven hundred wives and three hundred concubines, so that makes one wonder just a little about how wisdom is defined. Perhaps wisdom means "failing forward." This is a term that has endeared itself to me. It gives me permission to create a little stress and fail. Failing is okay. It takes all the stress out of being afraid to fail. Failing—I can do that. *Failing forward* simply means I have to learn from it and make a better decision next time. That's good. I can work with that theory.

Failing forward makes me totally able to do stupid things, like tap dancing (in the stretchy pants—yes, I think I've definitely decided to go with the stretchy pants). When this fails . . . and it probably will fail . . . then next time I'll just make a better decision. Next time I'll wear the pajama bottoms or try ballroom dance. Truth be told, the rope swing and deep ravine are looking better and better.

Drunk Chickens

When I was a little girl, every year my mom made me go down to the food storage room in the basement, haul out the cans that had gotten old, and empty all the bottled fruit that had spoiled. It was a smelly, gooey, nasty, sticky job. I hated it.

When Granny moved in with us a few years ago, we inherited her old food storage. I tried to leave most of it behind, but she insisted it was still good, and, well—I hated to hurt her feelings. So we boxed it up and packed it into my storage room. It might have remained forever hidden in the depths of my storage area except for one thing—we decided to move.

As we prepared to move, I decided I didn't feel sorry for Granny any more. I was not about to move that food storage one single inch. So I marched out to my storage room, started prying open lids, and began emptying all those rotten bottles of fruit. (I'm pretty sure it was fruit, but brown goo is brown goo, and it was pretty hard to tell.) I threw out all the cans that had gone bad and had popped lids. I threw out products I didn't like—such as apricots, for one.

I threw out a whole *case* of apricots. Nobody likes apricots. They're the guilt fruit—the "what if nothing else grows this year and there's a fruit shortage and this is all I have to eat for the whole winter?" fruit. If they ripened later in the season— say after the peaches, pears, pie cherries and plums—absolutely *nobody* would put up apricots. Even Granny doesn't like eating them—she just likes having them.

Granny also likes having cans of sauerkraut, Spam, dates, and pineapple. I found enough pineapple to make a native Hawaiian sick. NO ONE CAN EAT THAT MUCH PINEAPPLE. Apparently after several years of living with us, Granny didn't get the fact that no one in this house is going to make pineapple salad, pineapple cake, or pineapple anything else. And what did she think I was ever going to do with dates? Plug mice holes with them? She was a slow learner.

I started emptying all this fruit into buckets and dumping it out for the chickens. I ran across several bottles of very pungent fermented apples and fed those to the chickens, as well. The flies were getting drunk. The wasps were getting drunk. And, yes, the chickens had a whole lot to cackle about. Now, on a scale of one to ten, how much trouble am I in if I got my chickens drunk? I don't have a conscience about the flies and wasps. They grow up in cow pies. They deserve what they get. But I'm thinking those chickens might rat me out in heaven someday. There I'll be, strumming away at my harp, and some chicken will come up and peck a hole in the cloud.

Now, you're probably going to think this is a stretch (and what can I say—it is), but I'm including that little fruit-dumping episode in the "Something Physical" category. Why? Because I can. I make up the rules. I carried the jars from my storage room to the bucket, pried off the lids, shook the contents of the jars into the buckets, and hauled the buckets to the chickens. Then I went back for another load, and another, and another. It was physical, all right—just ask my shoulders. In fact, pretty much any time I discover muscles that I previously did not know existed, I count it as a physical exercise. In fact, because I laughed so hard at the wobbly chickens, I may just count it for two!

Something of Service

Magnanimous Acts

Students in the two-story brick country schoolhouse where I attended elementary school brought roller skates for a couple of weeks each spring and fall. They were the old adjustable skates that required a silver key to be lengthened or shortened, widened or tightened. They were held on partly by a leather strap around the ankle and mostly by good skating. That's why I had such a problem with them. I couldn't skate.

I was in second grade before I got to take a pair of skates to school. I was the fifth of ten children, and I didn't have skates until a sibling or two went on to junior high school. I was mighty proud when my turn finally came. I strapped those skates on and fumbled with the key until I got the clamps to bite down on my shoes and into my flesh. Then every recess for days I clung to the fence along the sidewalk, trying to roller-skate through the gravel. Every time, I ended up falling in a heap on the sidewalk, roller skates askew, picking gravel out of my kneecaps.

That all changed the day Carol found me. Carol was in sixth grade. She wasn't very well liked. Kids teased her for not being smart and for smelling bad. Her brother didn't help— he was always in fights, probably over the very same things. Carol's clothes were wrinkled and dirty, but she had a great smile. Carol found me in a heap one day picking gravel out of my knees yet again. She helped me get my skates back on and told me to hang on to her instead of the fence; she offered to walk beside me while I learned to skate. During that recess and several others, Carol propped me up. With her help I eventually learned to skate.

It didn't occur to me until I was grown why Carol was even available to help me—she didn't have skates of her own. I doubt her family could afford them. It didn't occur to me that maybe Carol wished she could have my skates, or maybe wished she could just use them. She never mentioned it, and as a second-grader, I certainly didn't pick up on any of that— I was concerned only about skating myself.

It wasn't Carol's fault that her family was poor. It wasn't Carol's fault that her clothes were wrinkled and dirty. It wasn't Carol's fault that she didn't have skates of her own. Carol had quite simply decided to be happy with her circumstances. Instead of resenting my good fortune, Carol was happy for me. Carol was willing to help someone who was more fortunate than herself without self-pity.

I kept one of my roller skate keys. Now, years later, it's in my story jar—the jar that contains reminders of what I want to tell the grandkids someday. I want to tell them about Carol and about people who happily see beyond their own needs to help others. Her act was magnanimous.

I saw another magnanimous act during my daughter's senior basketball season. My daughter's coach was Joel Bate. He was a great guy. He seemed to seek no personal acclaim or reputation. He simply wanted to do something he loved and help every girl achieve her potential, whatever that was. In his opinion, that was to take his girls to the state tournament. And he did. But I will not remember him for his basketball skill. I will remember him for something quite different.

The girls were playing basketball in the gym at another school. In that particular gym, benches for players and coaches were divided by a stair walkway. Spectators using the stair walkway constantly walked past our players on their way to the concession stand; as a result, our players kept moving back a little as people walked past so that no one was forced out onto the floor.

During that game, an older woman carefully made her way down the stairs. I watched her from the other side of the gym and was a little fearful that she would not be able to make it down the stairs without a handrail. Coach Bate was walking the sideline, trying not to step on his players or bump into the many spectators that walked by, when he caught sight of this woman out of the corner of his eye. By then she was on the bottom two or three steps.

It's crucial to realize that this coach was in the middle of a game. His girls were running up and down the floor, and he was doing his best to help them. But as Coach Bate caught sight of that woman coming down the last few steps, he immediately turned and offered her his arm. In that instant, he forgot the game so that other, more important things could be attended to.

A coach like that—a person who is a decent human being and a gentleman first—can coach a child of mine any day, regardless of what he knows about sports.

That act of charity, which went largely unnoticed, was magnanimous. I want to be like that. Carol and Joel are heroes to me, and I want to give someone else the great feeling they gave me. I want to be somebody's hero without recognition and without expecting personal gain.

Another person who knew about charity was Verna. I was assigned to visit teach Verna—who, quite frankly, I had *never* seen at church. She lived about forty miles away, and it took all of a morning or all of an afternoon to visit just her. I enjoyed our visits. She was kind and warm and welcoming and had the best throaty giggle. Eventually her husband joined our visits. I taught very little doctrine when I visited, but we enjoyed each other's company very much.

During the time I visited Verna I experienced some family trials. My family of ten brothers and sisters had customarily gathered quite often for holiday dinners, birthdays, and family home evenings. All of a sudden we stopped. Hard feelings had developed. Cousins didn't play with cousins. Aunts and uncles didn't speak. It was devastating.

I was extremely frustrated over the circumstances, and one night I dragged the garbage out to the burn barrel—even though that was my son's chore—because I needed to be alone. My tears fell freely as I struck the match and lighted the trash on fire. I did something then that I had never done before and don't plan on ever doing again: I kicked the burn barrel. Hard. This isn't the smartest thing to do for several reasons, not the least of which is that it hurts. Then I really *did* have a reason to cry, but I didn't care. I was already crying.

As I look back on my life, I can count the lowest of the low points on the fingers of one hand. That was one of them. We wouldn't be having holiday dinners any more. The cousins wouldn't grow up and build tree houses and have dirt clod fights together. Grandparents would not be able to watch their grandchildren grow up. This wasn't the way it was supposed to be.

During the months of hurt that followed, one act of charity sticks out in my mind more than any other. Many people knew about our family problems, but most simply didn't know what to do or say. I don't hold that against them. I didn't know what to do or say either. But Verna did. One afternoon that summer, Verna and her husband drove up to my house. They had been to town, which was about a 130-mile round trip for them. On their way home, they stopped at my house and parked their car under my poplar tree. Verna walked across the lawn and handed me a little German chocolate cake and a flowering cactus that she had purchased at the grocery store. She said something like, "I just wanted you to know I was thinking of you." Then she simply turned and left.

With five little kids the cake didn't last long; it was gone in moments. I don't know if Verna picked that cactus out for me on purpose, and I don't know if it had any significance other than its single beautiful bloom. The cactus became my . . . symbol, I guess. Our family difficulties were just like the cactus spines that poked me no matter how I handled it. I had certainly felt the pricks over the past months, and more pricks were coming—it was inevitable. Nonetheless, the cactus had a bloom. Its single beautiful yellow bloom was more beautiful, really, because of where it came from. I latched onto that symbolism with all my heart. In spite of my difficulties and the way I'd been pricked, I wanted to bloom someday.

I don't know what else Verna said, if she said anything at all. She just quietly drove away with her husband. Verna's sweet act of charity did more to heal my heart during that difficult time than anything anyone else had done.

Verna, Joel, and Carol—they are my heroes. I want to be just like them someday.

It's All About the Sacrifice

I believe in several things—one of which is trying to be nice. What a great service if people in this world would be a little nicer. Although I know not everyone is going to agree, I also believe in saving seats. It is almost impossible, of course, to be nice and save seats at the same time. That is why the state track finals left me in such turmoil.

I've been a seat saver since I was little: Dad perched me on a bench at stake conference and told me to save seats for the family. Since there were ten kids in our family, this was no small thing. I hated it, of course, but I didn't dare refuse. I learned that the trick to saving seats is being confident, bluffing everyone who comes along, and using every available coat, handbag, program, and coloring book to take up space. It also helps to put your hands on your hips as you stand.

I had lots of practice. Growing up I saved seats at rodeos, school concerts, football games, basketball games, and any other event you'd care to name. I still hated it, but at least I was good at it. You wouldn't believe how far I can make a diaper bag, a baseball cap, and a piano recital program stretch. But no matter how long I've done it, it still boils down to a battle of wills, and it's still stressful.

Sometimes saving even three or four seats is a strain, so you can imagine my stress one spring at having to save roughly forty seats. Yes—don't cringe—I said *forty*. It was the state championship track meet. My daughter was a senior and was competing in four running events. Fred and I had somehow been elected to save enough seats for the entire track team and the entourage of parents and supporters. Oh—and could we manage to save them right on the finish line . . . and in the shade—you know, for the sake of the team?

The stadium was to open at 8:00 that morning. We arrived at 7:15 and waited. At 7:30 the ticket takers arrived and set up camp. At 7:35 Fred talked them into letting us into the stadium because he had a pass. We looked like a couple of homeless people hauling all our worldly possessions up two seating levels. We had blankets, sweatshirts, newspapers, event programs, coolers, juice, sunscreen, movie cameras, 35mm cameras, hats, and grocery sacks full of apples, granola bars, chips, and Oreos—and roughly two hours to wait.

Saving places for forty people is tricky. Luckily we had enough stuff to cover a whole lot of bench, so the seats definitely looked like they were being saved, but obviously we couldn't cover every inch of metal. Still, any reasonable person could see that the seats were saved. When people started filling up the benches around us at 8:00, Fred and I stood up along the aisle seats, so that no one could mistake the fact that THE SEATS WERE SAVED. All was going well. Yes, we got a few sidelong glances that clearly implied, "How rude for you to take the very best seats in the stadium," but I had no problem ignoring these. We got there at 7:30. If they wanted good seats, they should have gotten to the stadium early instead of enjoying the continental breakfast at the motel. It's all about the sacrifice.

Our plan was working, until Fred left me! I had no idea where he went, but all of a sudden I turned around and he was gone. How dare he take a bathroom break at this crucial juncture! Had I known he needed to go to the bathroom I'd have been understanding—and then I'd have told him to hold it, for crying out loud, and take one for the team. But he didn't even give me the chance.

As I stood saving seats alone, I must not have looked very intimidating. Almost immediately three people started climbing over the benches to sit on one of the few spots of exposed metal. The nerve. The audacity. Well, they weren't going to get away with it. Not on my watch.

"Excuse me, sir. These seats are saved." He was about my age and roughly my weight (although I'm not proud of that); still, if confronted by him in a dark alley, I thought I could take him.

"You can't save seats." He didn't even look at me—as if I was a non-entity, a non-person, a non-component. Big mistake. Big. Huge. Little did he know he had just ticked off the wrong person.

"Yes, I can. I have been here since seven thirty. If you wanted good seats you should have come earlier. I came early." How was *that* for confrontation?

"You can't save seats."

"Look buddy, EVERYBODY here saves seats. All the teams save them. I'm saving them for our team—for the athletes."

"You can't save seats." Broken robot. Couldn't he come up with a more original argument?

"YES, I CAN. And what's more . . . I did. Clearly, you didn't."

He refused to argue. He refused to look at me. However, the young girl and the older gentleman with him nudged the man and said, "Come on, let's sit over there." And he ignored *them*, too. They were embarrassed by the confrontation and left—meekly, mildly, apologetically.

I tried again. "Sir, don't you think it's rude of you to take seats that were saved? I was here early. I paid the price. You didn't."

He ignored me. I was incensed. Fine, if he wanted to play

that way, then I'd just go get Fred. I turned around and, sure enough, here came Fred.

"Fred," I said to my knight in shining armor, "that man won't leave, and I've told him he's being rude and the seats were saved."

And my knight in shining armor said, "Well, there's nothing I can do about it." Nothing he could do about it? Fred had at least sixty pounds on the guy. I wanted him to use all sixty of it to intimidate—to bully. I wanted the man to feel fear. But there was nothing he could do about it? In that moment, his knight's armor seemed painfully thin to me—more like fish scales.

This was war. I know about war. I can write the book on war. If he goes low, I'll go lower. If he gets tricky, I'll get trickier. No man in this world can be more divisive than me. This guy had no idea what he was in for. This was personal now.

I waited for my grandsons to show up—a one-year-old and a three-year-old. Perfect. Of all thirty-nine saved seats, we sat down RIGHT NEXT to the man. I couldn't wait for the one-year-old to need a serious diaper change. In the meantime, I gave the kids every sticky snack I had, and I had plenty. Oops, spilled pop? Too bad. Oops, Oreo cookie stuck to your newspaper? Too bad. Oh, darn it, was that your camera case he put the orange peels in? Too bad. The kids crawled over and under and around him, and I let them. Their cars went under his legs and the kids crawled after them. Their bouncy balls hit him in the back of the head. Their tractors rammed his thighs. This would be a slow and painful death. We were more annoying than a mosquito in a phone booth, and his silly pride wouldn't let him open the door.

I probably sound like I'm gloating, but actually I'm not terribly proud of what happened. I used my grandkids as weapons. That's pretty low. Eventually I began to feel slightly

. . . slightly—oh, what's the right phrase here?—slightly pathetic? Lacking in honor and common decency? Lower than the mass of wet, rotten potatoes in my cellar? All very fitting. I wasn't proud of the fact that no matter how rude this guy was, I returned rudeness for rudeness. It almost felt like . . . like . . . like maybe . . . possibly . . . I should a . . . ap . . . apologize? Oh, heaven forbid! The thought made my stomach churn.

I rationalized that maybe this was the enabler in me coming through. If I ignored the guilt, maybe it would go away. On the other hand, maybe it was legitimately my conscience speaking. It's so hard to tell the difference. I analyzed it. Enabler or conscience; conscience or enabler? It didn't seem to matter. My stomach was doing flip-flops and I knew I couldn't live with this.

I approached him again. "Sir, I'm sorry I was rude earlier. I shouldn't have been rude." There; I had said my piece.

He finally looked at me and said, "Well, you can't save seats."

I was stunned. Is that all he could say? I offer an apology to meet him halfway, and that's all he has to say? I didn't say I was sorry for saving seats. I said I was sorry for being rude. How dare he imply I was sorry for saving seats? I bit my tongue, clenched my jaw, and refused to make eye contact with him.

Failing to get an admission of guilt from me, he repeated, "You can't save seats. It's not allowed."

Oh, he was *so* wrong. And oh, how I wanted to fight this war anew. I wanted to stomp on his newspaper. I wanted to spit on his shoe. I wanted to grind him beneath the heel of a very high stiletto shoe—which I didn't own but would buy that very day. I wanted to write a war motto on his forehead in lipstick. I wanted him to know without a doubt that I was not apologizing for saving seats, but only for being rude—and I desperately wanted him to know the difference. I wanted him to know he was out-matched, out-gunned, out-skilled, and seriously out-scored. I wanted him to eat pond scum.

But for the sake of being "nice," I did not open my big mouth. I did the hard thing. I—just—shut—up. And I just about exploded. Sister Margaret Nadauld said, "Women of God can never be like women of the world. The world has enough women who are tough; we need women who are tender. There are enough women who are coarse; we need women who are kind. There are enough women who are rude; we need women who are refined. We have enough women of fame and fortune; we need more women of faith. We have enough greed; we need more goodness. We have enough vanity; we need more virtue. We have enough popularity; we need more purity." ("The Joy of Womanhood," *Ensign,* Nov. 2000, 14.)

She's right. We don't need women who can save forty seats with nastiness. We need women who can save thirty-nine seats with kindness, grace, and generosity. It's all about the sacrifice.

Mount McKinley

When my daughter was in fifth grade, the teacher assigned a science experiment. Students were to search the milkweed plants along the ditch banks until they found a Monarch butterfly caterpillar. They were to put the caterpillar in a jar with a stick and milkweed leaves, and they were to provide fresh leaves every day until the caterpillar formed its cocoon.

We jumped on this project with great energy, and the whole family helped search for the caterpillar. After a few days of munching on milkweed leaves in the jar, the caterpillar dutifully formed its cocoon on the stick. It was beautiful—the same green as the milkweed plant with a golden thread around the top. It really was a masterpiece. We anxiously awaited the transformation of the caterpillar into a butterfly.

A few days passed. No butterfly. A few more days passed, and the cocoon began to look brown and dry. I was worried that our caterpillar had actually rotted. Soon, it looked worse. It began to resemble the dried umbilical cord of a two-week-old baby. It was disgusting.

I was sure we had done something wrong, and that the cocoon was slowly disintegrating. I was right: it was disintegrating, but that wasn't a bad thing. A few days later, the butterfly had emerged. It was incredibly colored and detailed and perfect.

We took the jar outside to set our butterfly free. The kids and I expected that when we opened the jar, the butterfly would fly away. It didn't. It just sat there like it had a tummy ache. Once again I thought we had done something wrong. Our butterfly was defective. The kids tried to be patient. We waited and waited. We nudged it a little—okay, a lot. But the butterfly didn't seem terribly interested in flying. It would go a foot or two and then quit. I expected its wings to be strong right away. I didn't realize that being cramped in a dried umbilical cord for two weeks had not made the wings strong.

The kids and I finally got tired of encouraging the butterfly to fly and of trying to keep the dogs away from it. So we took it out outside the fenced yard, put it on some weeds, and left it alone. When we went back later to see if it was there, it was gone. We like to think it finally took flight.

It still sort of amazes me. Out of something so small came something so incredible. Through a slow but constant process of change, something really spectacular emerged.

Mt. McKinley is like that. Mt. McKinley (locally called Denali) is located in Denali National Park in Alaska. It is 20,320 feet high—so high, in fact, that it creates its own weather, plummeting the temperature as low as 95 degrees below zero Fahrenheit, and creating winds of 100 to 150 miles per hour. Mt. McKinley is so high that on a clear day it can be seen from as far as 600 miles away.

Nearly 1,000 people a year try to climb Mt. McKinley, usually in June. The total round-trip hiking distance is 46 miles, and 13,000 feet of the climb is vertical. If the climber makes it to the top, mental capacity at that elevation is reduced by two-thirds!

The core of Mt. McKinley is granite, and it was formed by two tectonic plates pushing against each other, forcing the granite through the earth's crust. The fascinating thing to me is that the mountain grew at the average rate of only four to six millimeters (less than a quarter-inch) per year. My toenails grow faster than that. It's amazing to think of such a gradual, constant, steady, and incremental process. Out of something extremely small came something amazingly incredible. Through a slow but constant process of change emerged something spectacular.

Geologists say that those quarter-inch increases began more than sixty-five million years ago. Can you imagine being tasked with "measuring the mountain's growth"? How silly would that have seemed? I wonder how long I would have lasted.

I'm not fond of increments. I prefer giant leaps. I would really like it if things came all at once. But one thing I have learned is that things of real value tend to come incrementally. Here's one way to look at it:

"For behold, thus saith the Lord God: I will give unto the children of men line upon line, precept upon precept, here a little and there a little; and blessed are those who hearken unto my precepts, and lend an ear unto my counsel, for they shall learn wisdom; for unto him that receiveth I will give more; and from them that shall say, We have enough, from them shall be taken away even that which they have." (2 Ne. 28:30.)

The same principle is emphasized in the Doctrine and Covenants:

"But all things must come to pass in their time.

"Wherefore, be not weary in well-doing, for ye are laying the foundation of a great work. And out of small things proceedeth that which is great." (D&C 64:32–33.)

And again in Alma:

"Now ye may suppose that this is foolishness in me; but behold I say unto you, that by small and simple things are great things brought to pass; and small means in many instances doth confound the wise.

"And the Lord God doth work by means to bring about his great and eternal purposes; and by very small means the Lord doth confound the wise and bringeth about the salvation of many souls." (Alma 37:6–7.)

Remember the story of Moses leading the children of Israel out of Egypt? One of his first dilemmas was how to feed them; in response, the Lord sent manna, symbolizing the spiritually sustaining bread of life or love of God. There was a condition, however. Manna had to be gathered each day. If the gatherers collected enough manna to last for more than one day, it could not be stored successfully; more manna had to be gathered the next day. The exception was Sunday: Saturday's efforts could be stored for one extra day, sparing the children of Israel from laboring on the Sabbath.

It must have been a tedious process—gathering only a little at a time. Yet it contributed to the incremental spiritual growth of the children of Israel—a process that would require them to rely on the Lord. It took forty years for them to mature spiritually. Compared to Mt. McKinley and its sixty-five million years of growth, forty years seems rather speedy—unless, of course, you're the gatherer.

We are all gatherers. We visit sisters in our wards every month, bringing them a little manna—a little of the love of God. Last month's visit doesn't negate our need to serve again this month. A really good visit this month won't hold over. We must bring the love of the Lord into the lives of the sisters we visit one day at a time, one week at a time, one month at a time. And that gradual, consistent, incremental accumulation of the Lord's love will eventually help these sisters to rise to their potential in the Lord's fold.

I've heard some women say that they don't need to visit Sister So-and-So because she's active and comes to church and knows the gospel. The truth is, active sisters need that manna on a regular basis, just as anyone else does. They need the love of the Lord brought to them.

I don't know how many women I've visited over the past twenty-five-plus years as a visiting teacher. Most were less-active members. I wanted so badly to see progress and growth in these women while I visited them. I wanted them to have the blessings of the priesthood in their homes. I wanted them to enjoy the blessings of making and keeping covenants. I wanted them to have the peace and comfort that the gospel brings. I wanted them to have confidence in the Atonement. It strikes me now as ironic that these women and my service to them—and your service as a visiting teacher—is very similar to the manna that must come daily, weekly, monthly. It must be constant, gradual, and incremental in order to get that Mt. McKinley of a spirit to rise in strength and confidence. Yet look at the mountain that resulted from years of less than one-quarter-inch growth at a time. And eternity is a long time—lots longer than sixty-five million years.

The late Mother Teresa said: "We must not drift away from the humble works, because these are the works nobody will do. It is never too small. We are so small, we look at things in a small way, but God, being Almighty, sees everything great; therefore, even if you write a letter for a blind man, or you just go and sit and listen, or you take the mail for him, or you visit somebody, or bring a flower to somebody, small things, or wash clothes for somebody, or clean the house, very humble work, that is where you and I must be. For there are many people who can do big things, but there are very few people who will do the small things. Our loaves and fishes can feed thousands; give Jesus not only your hands to serve, but your heart to love. Pray with absolute trust in God's loving care for you. Let him use you without consulting you. Let Jesus fill you with joy that you may preach without preaching."

As we bring the love of the Lord into the lives of our sisters, our service as visiting teachers is also similar to manna. We love the gospel and want to see its effects in the lives of those we love. We are impatient; we want results NOW! I want so much to see the sisters that I visit gain stronger testimonies, yet year after year their growth can seem so small, so indiscernible, that it appears there might be none at all.

It's easy to become discouraged when we try to chart progress from our mortal perspective. It's easy to become discouraged with visiting teaching if we don't see results, if we don't feel friendships forming, if we don't think our efforts are appreciated or even wanted, and if we sometimes feel annoyed at the inconvenience. It's easy to feel that we have no effect at all. Yet for most intents and purposes, the gospel "distills" on us in nearly indiscernible increments through our monthly visits to each other, our weekly contacts at church, and our daily prayers on behalf of each other. Few perspectives have been more helpful to me than to remember that the Lord's love "distills" upon us as manna, and that manna comes daily.

Please don't give up on me or on the sisters you visit. Our growth is small, sometimes indiscernible—but our *potential* for growth is great.

One Love

A person should really have only one love in her life. I have strayed. I love my husband, to whom I am married for eternity, but for some inexplicable reason I also love chickens. We could analyze this, but really, are chickens worth the effort? What would be the point? And yet, you know I can't resist.

Why do I love chickens? Theory one: Chickens are a tie to my agricultural roots. I miss the farm. I miss hearing the hay baler thumping away in the early morning. I miss the tractors circling the fields. I miss the smell of cows and horses. I miss the smell of dirt. I miss . . . well, no, I guess I really don't miss the spud digger. There's just no way to romanticize a spud digger and the smell of water rot under my fingernails. There's no way to pretend that it wasn't unbearable and dangerous. That's not the only thing I don't miss. I hated picking cockleburs out of my socks and pants. And I hated riding in the hills to gather cows in the hot afternoon sun— that was torture. I hated being yelled at during branding time; yeah, I don't really miss that. So much for theory one.

Theory two: Chickens require no emotional attachment and can therefore suck no energy from you. Chickens cannot disobey their owner's commands as a dog can, because chickens were never trained to obey. You don't pet a chicken; if you do, you get pecked. You also can't emotionally attach to anything that can't make eye contact with you. A chicken can't do that: its face is just too narrow. You'll go cross-eyed trying. That's not all: if a dog or a cat or a fish dies, people feel the need to have a funeral. If a chicken dies, we think, "Ooh, ooh, can we save the meat?" Theory two is definitely in the running.

Theory three: Chickens are productive. A little corn, a little wheat, and *voilà*—we have the extremely useful and versatile egg. Sure, there's a little manure to clean up, but chickens don't require laundering or ironing. On the other hand, I can feed my husband a little corn, a little wheat, and he'll sit and watch TV all evening. Not useful. Not versatile. And he'll definitely still want clothes laundered and ironed.

Theory four: Chickens need me. My children are grown, and if I didn't answer my phone for a few days, they'd live. I'm replaceable. But my chickens—if I left them for a day or two they'd be in a panic. They'd be desperate. I need someone to miss me desperately. This is pathetic, I know, but I need to be needed.

Theory five: Chickens fascinate me. How does a chicken decide which nest to lay eggs in? I have fifteen laying hens and a dozen nesting boxes, yet all the hens lay eggs in just two of the boxes. The other ten boxes sit empty. This fascinates me. The other ten laying boxes have great little piles of clean wood shavings in them. Don't they want their own spots? Their own boxes? Their privacy? Do they just use the same box because it's already warm, and who wants to sit on cold wood shavings? Do you suppose they line up and take turns in the box? They must—they can't all sit in the box at once. So laying eggs must not be like going to the bathroom, because who could wait long enough for chicken number nine to lay? That's got to be like a chicken bathroom line nightmare. Then there is the odd hen who skips the box entirely and lays her egg right on the floor. Maybe she couldn't wait for the box. This would support the bathroom line theory.

Now let's look at this. My first love, my husband, is not tied to my agricultural roots. Chickens are. Husband—0, Chickens—1. My husband requires emotional attachment, which can suck the energy right out of me. Chickens require no such energy. On the other hand, my husband can make eye contact with me, but chickens only make me go cross-eyed. Husband—1, Chickens—1. My husband is productive but requires a little more than corn and wheat. Chickens are productive, but I can't live on eggs alone. (Actually, my husband is much more productive.) Husband—2, Chickens—1. Chickens need me but are not loyal; anyone who gives them corn and wheat will do. My husband needs me—he just doesn't know how much. My husband is much more loyal, I hope. Husband—3, Chickens—1. My husband is not as fascinating. He'll tell me exactly what he thinks—straight up. Chickens, on the other hand, leave so much to my imagination. They refute none of my theories. They peck at my toes—why do they do this? They are truly fascinating. Husband—3, Chickens—2.

Well, there you have it. My husband won by a nose (or feather).

The day my husband and I went to the Ogden Utah Temple to be sealed, it could be that he resembled a chicken. He was scrawny. I thought he was handsome, of course, but tall and thin . . . no, *scrawny* pretty well sums it up. And he needed me. It's hard to resist someone who needs you. But why do I stay with him? . . . *That* is the question.

Theory one: My husband (just like the chickens) was a tie to my agricultural roots because he grew up working on his family ranch.

Theory two: My husband (just like the chickens) requires far less emotional attachment than I had originally thought. If he is fed and has a recliner, newspaper, and remote control, he needs very little else from me. He had relatively few feelings to share when we first married, and nothing much has changed on that front. Can his psyche be so simple? Yes, I'm afraid so.

Theory three: My husband (just like the chickens) is productive. He brings home a paycheck every month. Give him a little Tin Roof Sundae ice cream and occasional crab legs, and he's really quite content to put a mulching kit on the lawnmower (albeit backwards), build shelves in the storage room, move the cans of dry-pack food storage eight times, and still bring home the paycheck. Yes, he's productive.

Theory four: My husband (like the chickens) needs me. Who would feed him vegetables? Who would explain that ketchup is not a food group? Who would trim his ear hairs?

Theory five: My husband fascinates me. He throws Tootsie Rolls that are still in their wrappers to the dogs because they love to eat them. Did you know a dog cannot unwrap the candy? My husband doesn't care. This fascinates me. How can one throw candy IN THE WRAPPER to the dog, then sit and watch the dog eat it? My husband also believes that he could build a hay baler with a little duct tape and a pair of pliers. Isn't that fascinating—and a little scary at the same time?

The other day, my son Will came home from an office supply store where he had been buying folders and binders and other things with which to organize his new business. As he was showing his wife, Erica, his new purchases, he said, "Oh, and I bought some stuff for you, too." He reached in his packages and drew out some scrapbooking papers and stickers; he remembered that Erica had been trying to get their wedding pictures put in a book. I was reminded again of what a tender heart Will has and what a good husband he'll be, because he always thinks of others. He got that from his dad. For my last birthday, Fred wanted to buy me a nice free-standing cupboard where I could keep goodies for the grandkids when they came to visit. He hunted around town and couldn't find one that was built well enough at a low enough price to suit him. So he bought the wood and spent the next three Saturdays in his shop making a cupboard for me. It's that giving, not-about-me heart that I find so endearing. What's not to love?

What it comes down to is this: my husband has charity. My chickens do not. My husband *is* charity. Charity is a state of being, not a single action. Charity is *what we are* rather than *what we do*. I want to be more like that. I want to *be* that.

What does all of this mean? (So glad you asked.) This means that if I got really desperate and had to give up one—chickens or husband—I would give up the chickens.

Fred will be so glad to hear that.

ChristMas Spirit

While most people are out Christmas shopping, wondering what to buy and what not to buy—and, more importantly, which credit card to buy it with—I am relegated to the aisles of the hardware store. Hardware stores don't even bother to put up tissue-paper bells or paint their windows with curlicues and holly. And I can positively attest that there is no Christmas spirit in the bathroom fixtures aisle.

Santa started a construction project in my basement one fall and was almost finished with the bathroom by the time Christmas approached, so Santa personally took me on a shopping trip to the hardware store to buy the fixtures. How hard can that be, right? Well, harder than you think. Did you know you have to buy the toilet bowl separate from the tank? They don't come together? What were the little toilet elves thinking? Who needs a bowl without a tank? Or a tank without a bowl? What if you had a bowl but no tank, or vice versa? Hello! Then I found you also have to buy the toilet *seat* separately. What's up with that? Who planned this whole toilet scam?

I'll tell you who: the same elves who boxed up the vanity cabinet separate from the sink-top unit. Like I'm ever going to need a vanity with a huge hole in the top. I'm thinking there was a little too much eggnog flowing at the North Pole when the elves who were bored with Spiderman action figures thought up the sinkless vanity. A sinkless vanity rates right up there on the gift list with fruitcake.

We loaded our purchases in our Ford sleigh and the next night Santa began assembling the bathroom cabinet. He drilled and hammered, and I even saw him use a measuring tape once, so I thought things were going quite well—until I heard him say, "The directions are WRONG." (Actually, I was quite impressed that he even looked at the directions.)

No wonder the elves do the assembling up north. I'll bet they don't let Santa touch the electrical wiring, either. Last week we couldn't get our furnace to run and we were freezing. Strangely enough, Santa had done some wiring on the downstairs bathroom about that same time. Let's see—Santa working on the wiring, furnace not working—Santa working on the wiring, furnace not working—Santa working on the wiring . . . do we see a pattern here?

My daughter and I wrapped up in blankets and insisted to Santa that THERE'S A PROBLEM. Finally, he called our friendly furnace elf to come and see what was wrong with the furnace, and guess what he found? Somebody had been messing with the wiring. Go figure.

Santa has plenty of Christmas spirit and his heart is in the right place but it's time somebody tells him—he shouldn't quit his day job.

I've gone into the Christmas season way too many times with just this kind of attitude—uninspired. That's why I keep the letter my sister Rachel wrote to another of my sisters. Here it is.

> Dear Jane,
> One great thing about Christmas was a gift that Cache [age twelve] got me. We drew names a couple of weeks ago, and Cache finagled it until he got mine. We took turns

opening the presents, and it finally got to me. I opened the bag and there was a Scout shirt on top. Cache hadn't had time to wrap it. In fact, we had to wait while he found something to put my present in. I thought the Scout shirt was just to cover what was inside. I pulled it out and found another Scout shirt underneath, and another one under that, and two sashes below that. It dawned on me by about the third shirt—Cache had taken everybody's Scout shirts and all of the badges he could find, and had hand-sewn each and every one of them where they should go. I didn't even have the troop number sewn on them. (At one time I stapled one on, but it fell off.)

I started to tear up. It was the sweetest, most thoughtful thing. I kept telling the kids I would sew the badges on. I knew it was important to them, I just couldn't seem to find any extra time, but I told them I would spend the whole week after Christmas doing it. Justin [age fourteen] said that every night Bert and I went on a date, Cache would sneak out the Scout shirts and badges and work and work on them while we were gone. This has gone on for more than three months. Cache would get so frustrated he would throw them aside and say, "I give up." Justin said, "Everybody would always tell him how good he was doing, and not to give up. Sometimes Jesse [age ten] would help him rip them out so he could start over." Cache finally got all but one sash done, and he wrapped them up for me for Christmas. I tell you, I should write my own tear-jerker Christmas book. What a kid. What a great kid. What great kids to cheer him on. And not one whisper of it to me. Even when he couldn't find the one and only needle in the house for two weeks! Amazing. And very, very humbling.

    Love,
    Rachel

Well, thanks to my nephew Cache, I will try harder this year to keep the "Spirit" in "Christmas spirit," and I will remember to really serve someone.

The Story Jar

"Mom, tell me a story about when you were a little girl."

As my children grew up, I dreaded hearing that plea. I was never good at telling stories. Nothing in my life was interesting enough. I had sisters who were great storytellers, but I was not.

"Well, honey, I grew up on a farm. There really isn't much to tell. We grew potatoes. We also had cows. That's pretty much it. Why don't you ask Dad to tell you a story? Or maybe I could read you a book." The kids were distracted easily enough. But here's what broke my heart: after a while they quit asking me.

Then one day I was cleaning out my cedar chest. I found an elementary school play script, a bottle of canal water, a jade pendant, a roller skate key, tarnished earrings, dried rose petals, an event badge, an embroidered handkerchief with crocheted edging, satin baby booties, a letter, a silk corsage, and an old perfume bottle. There were so many little items—some were squished together and others were dangling loosely, threatening to get lost among all the dolls, blankets, and baby clothes.

Each item represented a little snatch of the past. I gathered them up—my treasures. But what could I do with them? No one ever saw them or appreciated them but me. No one else knew what episode or chapter they represented.

I took an old gallon milk jar and put each little item from my cedar chest in the jar. All those bits of memorabilia didn't fill a one-gallon jar, but they were colorful and oddly interesting. I set the jar on my dresser for weeks, admiring the eclectic display, knowing that it wouldn't bring even fifty cents at a yard sale—not that I would ever think of parting with it. And then one day as I looked at the jar I heard a young imaginary voice inside my head pleading, "Grandma, tell me a story about when you were a little girl." And Grandma's story jar was born.

Suddenly, I had a way to tell a story. I could tell the grandkids about the old perfume bottle and about my own grandmother, who helped me collect odd little bottles. I could tell them how I tried to walk on water just like the Apostle Peter, and when that didn't work, how I tried to muster enough faith to move that perfume bottle on my dresser. Then I would tell them about what faith really is and why God doesn't always do what we ask Him to.

Someday I will pull out of the story jar the little diamond-shaped, tarnished earrings of repentance. I will tell them that Grandpa and Grandma had only been married a few months, and Grandma found a new recipe; she fixed a nice casserole for Grandpa's lunch before they went to town that day. Grandpa came in for lunch, took one look at the casserole, swore, and said he wasn't about to eat that.

Grandma got really mad because she was trying to be a good wife and trying hard to learn to cook—and Grandpa wasn't helping! Grandma decided she'd fix him—she took the casserole out in the yard, fed it to the dog, and told Grandpa he could fix his own lunch. Then she went in her bedroom and cried.

Grandpa left the house mad—and hungry. He went to town without Grandma, but she didn't care. She didn't want to go to town any more.

When Grandpa returned home hours later, he wasn't mad any more. He walked in the door and handed Grandma a little box. Inside the box was nestled a pair of bright little diamond-shaped silver earrings—the same now-tarnished silver earrings inside the story jar.

Grandma was so happy with the earrings. She'd never had anything so pretty. She was even happier when Grandpa apologized about swearing at her casserole. And Grandpa never complained about Grandma's cooking ever again—not for the whole rest of their lives. He ate any old casserole or leftover or burnt roast she fixed. And one day years later, they had a good laugh over it—and over the fact that after the dog ate that first casserole, he threw up on the grass.

There are so many stories in the jar. They're just little stories. They are not really stories about the objects in the jar. Instead, they are stories of the values and experiences that make me who I am—stories of faith, compassion, repentance, obedience, hard times, prayer, and integrity. It's a jar that I can use to serve my grandkids.

"Grandma, tell me a story of when you were a little girl."

"Oh, honey, run and get the story jar. Have I told you about the tithing chickens yet?"

Mom's Gift

Mom is going to miss corn on the cob season this year—along with fresh garden tomatoes and red potatoes. Just two days before she passed away she asked me if the apricots were ready yet. I think this was her favorite time of year; she just loved all the fresh fruit and vegetables.

During the six years she lived with our family, Mom repeatedly told me she didn't want to be a burden. She was truly afraid that she might burden us. She had agreed to live with us only because her eyesight was failing and she was afraid of falling.

"Mom, it's no problem. I don't mind," I told her every time she brought it up.

I'll admit, I hadn't pictured this role for myself, but I really didn't mind it. Mom required very little care. We initially assumed she would incorporate into our family life, but I suppose she had lived by herself too long to really want to take part. She just wanted a place to put her bed, a rocking chair, a television, and a cupboard for her chocolate, and she was satisfied. There were trips to various doctors and occasional trips to town so she could shop, but for the most part she was very content. She didn't ask for much.

I don't want to make it sound as though there were never challenges—there were. She was once so mad at me she didn't speak for at least a week. She resented my management of her medication. Sometimes I didn't respond to a request as enthusiastically as she wanted.

We certainly had trying days when we tried to shop for groceries together. Her method was to shuffle up and down every single aisle and pick up absolutely anything that caught her fancy. This drove me nuts. I had lists. I had schedules. I had plans. A grocery store trip never took me more than fifteen minutes tops—and then only if there was a line at the checkout. Mom, on the other hand, easily passed an hour and a half in the grocery aisles and was still surprised when I told her it was time to go. She then wanted to follow that up with a trip to a bakery, a candy store, and a local produce stand—as if she forgot something! I wanted efficiency. She wanted to enjoy the moment. I was always in a rush. She had all day.

"Mom, what are you doing with those magazines?"

"I'm picking out seeds for the garden."

"You mean you're going to put perfectly good seeds in my weed patch? You'll give my weeds a complex."

"We'll do better this year."

"We?" This was another point of frustration. Her intentions were good. I'm not sure whether she actually intended to get out there and help or whether she was determined to make me a gardener, but she was mistaken on both counts. Nonetheless, she ordered seeds in the early spring every year and made a trip to the greenhouse to purchase flowers every spring—without fail. Gobs of flowers. An indecent amount of flowers. They offered punch-cards for flower purchases, and Mom filled her punch-card in one visit. The nurserymen loved to see her coming.

"Mom, we only have four flower barrels. You have too many flowers. They won't all fit."

"We could put some . . ." and she'd name every single place bordering the house or bordering the walkways or bordering the driveways or even bordering not much of anything. She insisted on sweet peas, bachelor buttons, dianthus, pansies, marigolds, geraniums, and five varieties of daisies. Every year she bought hollyhocks and every year I quietly dumped them over the fence. I know that wasn't nice, but Mom's memory was short. She never remembered buying them, and hollyhocks spread like thistle, so I really didn't want them around.

"Who's going to water the flowers and weed the gardens?" I asked.

"Oh, I'll help," she always assured me.

Sure she would. I have no doubt she intended to help, just like she intended to cook all the groceries she bought. I planted and planted and planted the flowers, and then I planted some more. Finally, I gave a bunch of them away. After all, it was the planning and the shopping that she enjoyed most. The rest was just details. She would have loved the bouquets that neighbors and friends sent to her funeral. They were so gorgeous, with pink-, lavender-, and salmon-colored blooms—just as she had always pictured them in her flower garden.

And then the day came when we called the family together in a hospital room where Mom was quickly fading. For about thirty hours we held Mom's hand, combed her hair, whispered that we loved her, and wished we could ease her suffering. By morning she had slipped into a coma. Just before noon, as the family gathered in her hospital room, Mom quietly slipped away. One moment there was breath; the next moment there was not.

For two weeks family visited, and we received amazing food gifts and flower arrangements and plant baskets. I talked to siblings and Relief Society sisters every day. The mailman never arrived without a handful of sympathy cards. People shared with us their love, tears, and support in the sweetest, gentlest ways. Each hug and smile made it a little easier. Each card and phone call gave us a chance to recall good friendships. Each bouquet reminded us of the beauty of life. Each tear reminded us of the compassion of others. It was a precious time.

I have no great epiphanies about mourning and loss. I have only random thoughts that as yet are a little disjointed. I don't have to figure all that out, though, to know that it was a blessing to our family to have Mom live with us. She gave us all an opportunity to grow.

The funeral flowers faded. We went back to work and resumed our lives, only now it was different. There seemed to be a soft blanket on mine. Not a heavy wool blanket, not a light linen sheet, just a moderate lap robe—just enough to remind me it was there. It was a blanket of sadness. I didn't have to monitor medication any more. I didn't have to determine if Mom had eaten something other than pretzels and chocolate. I didn't have to check her for bruises to see if she had fallen. I didn't have to ask if she needed anything from town. I didn't have to check the calendar to see if she had doctor's appointments. I didn't have to pull off the thick hose that kept her ankles from swelling. I didn't have to find the animal channel on her TV or explain for the billionth time how to use her two remote controls. Soon I will need to box up Mom's things; I will need to figure out what to keep and what to give away.

I picked a handful of cherry tomatoes and the first garden tomato this week. The first sweet corn of the season is ready now, and it will taste wonderful with the apricot cobbler I made. The early apples have already dropped from the tree, and it's time to collect seeds from the daisies. The summer days have started to cool. And I miss her.

"Oh, I don't want to be a burden to you."

"It's okay, Mom. I really don't mind."

Things Haven't Changed a Lick

My second son, Will, was a blond wanderer. He was a confident little thing at the age of four or five, and I'd have to send his older brother or sister out to find him at least twice a day. They usually found him on his way to see his dad on the farm somewhere, and they dragged him back for me, tears streaming down his face.

We lived in a remote little corner of Idaho at the time, and I didn't worry about traffic mangling him or people absconding with him. I *did* worry about the irrigation ditches, snakes, stock trucks, and tractors (if he made it that far). Will, however, was always convinced that his dad needed him, and he just had to oblige. For him the attempt was worth whatever spanking resulted.

Like most little boys, Will also had a wonderful gift for dreams. Whenever he hit a home run in Little League, he confidently looked to see if a newspaper reporter had made it to his game. He could stick a piece of tape on the living room wall for a basket and spend all morning as basketball star Michael Jordan, shooting a wad of rolled-up socks; he won countless championship rings and gave lots of TV interviews. In fact, I'm convinced Will "won" more medals and awards in his head than the whole NBA combined. I loved tucking him in at night just to hear what new thing his imagination had created.

Imagination is a good thing—most of the time. Occasionally, though, it backfires. One spring night when Will was about seven, I went to tuck him in and found him very troubled. He had a track meet the next day, and although I'm sure he had imagined himself crossing the finish line first in every single race, he had also imagined himself losing. I sat on the edge of his bed.

"Will, what's wrong?"

He was hesitant. "What if I don't do good tomorrow?"

I knew Will would see right through any platitudes I might offer. I couldn't tell him that winning didn't matter. Winning matters when you're seven. When you're seven years old, in bed and feeling the security of a nice quilt, then advice like "Just do your best" might work—for a while. But when your friends are receiving ribbons and everyone is cheering for them, a nice quilt isn't going to cut it.

It's a good thing that when a psychologist isn't handy, moms have access to a little thing called inspiration that makes us sound so smart. The rest of our conversation that night went something like this:

"Will, what color are your eyes?"

He looked at me as if to say, Haven't you been listening? Not knowing what else to do but participate, he answered, "Blue."

"What color are my eyes?" I asked.

"Blue."

"What's your dad's name?"

"Fred."

"Does he love you?"

"Yes."

"How many brothers do you have?"

"Two."

"What's my name?"

"Lynn."

"Do I love you?"

"Yes."

"What's Grandma's name?"

He had to think about that one, but he finally came up with, "Thelma."

"Does she love you?"

"Yes."

"What's at the top of the temple?"

"The angel Moroni."

"Will, if you lose the race tomorrow and come in dead last, what color will your eyes be?"

"Blue."

"What color will my eyes be?"

"Blue."

"What will your dad's name be?"

"Fred."

"Will he still love you?"

"Yes."

"How many brothers will you have?"

"Two."

"If everybody at the whole school finishes the race before you do, what will my name be?"

"Lynn."

"Will I still love you?"

"Yes."

"What will Grandma's name be?"

"Thelma."

"Will Grandma still love you?"

"Yes."

"What will still be at the top of the temple?"

"The angel Moroni."

"Then no matter what happens tomorrow—even if you don't win a single ribbon and even if every kid in the school finishes the race before you—tomorrow night I'll still tuck you in bed and tell you that I love you, and the things that are really important will still be the same. They won't change a lick. You will still like living on the farm. You will still wander out to find your dad."

He seemed to relax then, and soon he was asleep.

The next day at the track meet Will lined up with about twenty other seven-year-olds. When the whistle blew, he ran for all he was worth. When you line up twenty kids for a race, they quickly get pretty spread out. So since no one was near him when he crossed the finish line, Will figured he won, just as I'm sure he'd pictured it in his head a hundred times.

Thank heaven for small acts of service like tucking a child in at night. Actually, though, what happened that night—and the next day—was my child's service to me, not mine to him. That's the interesting part of serving—you can't give without receiving. It's simply not possible.

Epitaph

I went to a funeral the other day. It lasted two hours. I know funerals are emotional times during which we share memories, but two hours? We heard about every favorite food of the deceased and every one of his favorite television shows. Is that really helping the mourning process?

I have another small problem with Church funerals in particular, and I'm going to share it at the risk of stepping on a few toes. It seems we as Church members feel that when we get a few non-members within the walls of a meetinghouse for a funeral, we must address the Plan of Happiness—which is entirely appropriate. But for some reason we don't trust the Holy Ghost to testify of the truthfulness of that plan—so we club our captive audience over the head with it repeatedly. After two hours—trust me on this one—no one is listening.

I will now pause a moment for your rebuttal. I certainly don't expect everyone to agree. I'll even give you some ammunition with which to shoot it down—namely, "This lady has no idea what she's talking about whatsoever." True, all true.

My experiences with death have been very limited. And my experiences with the death of close loved ones have been even more so. Couple that with the fact that I grew up on a farm. Things died. Sometimes we even helped them die. We regularly butchered cows, chickens, and wild game. Even pets died all the time; I thought that's what pets were supposed to

do. I took 4-H for ten years. I started with pigs, then gradu-
ated to beef steers. But there is really only one reason to raise
a market pig or a market steer, and I'll give you one guess
what that reason is. So death was not just part of the process,
it *was* the process. I don't even remember crying over it.
Really, who needs to be responsible for feeding and watering
an animal all winter? It might be okay for summer, but
winter? Good riddance.

This has no doubt influenced my perspective. Nonetheless,
setting aside this whole animal thing, two hours is still too
long for a funeral, and I still don't think knowing what the
deceased person's favorite food is can help the mourning
process.

I went to a funeral a few years ago for an elderly widow I
had met only once, and it was the best funeral I've ever been
to. I went to the funeral to support her daughter, who was my
friend.

The bishop gave the deceased woman the nicest tribute
I've ever heard. He said the woman had held several positions
in the ward and had always been diligent in her responsibili-
ties. When the woman was about eighty-three years old, he
called her to be the Sunbeam teacher. She responded that she
was getting older and couldn't get up and down very well any
more, but if the Lord wanted her to do it, then she'd try. The
bishop went on to say that this woman was probably the most
beloved Sunbeam teacher they'd ever had.

After a few years of being the Sunbeam teacher, the
bishop asked if she would accept a calling to work in the ward
library. She responded that she was getting older and didn't
know if she could remember where things were, but if the
Lord wanted her to do it, then she'd try. The bishop went on
to explain that this woman served faithfully in that calling
and was there every Sunday until her health declined and she
could no longer attend meetings.

I remember sitting in this woman's funeral thinking, "This is how I hope to live. I hope I live in such a way that when I die, I will have been found serving until my very last breath. That's all." Does anything else matter?

(And just for future reference, if my family can't promise to keep my funeral under an hour, then I'm calling in the Protestants to do it.)

I'm the Mother, I Think

People are always saying that mothers give service all the time. My oldest daughter Jenny and I were arguing the other day about who Rachel's mother is. Technically, Rachel is the youngest of my children. She came at the cost of a C-section, so I unmistakably remember bringing her into this world.

But Rachel pretty much always preferred Jenny over me. Jenny had kind, loving arms that were unhurried and gentle. I only had one arm to give Rachel, and it was always moving rather quickly in a spanking motion. My other arm was constantly reaching for one of her brothers to pull him out of the dishwasher or to keep him from falling off the deck or to keep him out of the cake batter.

Jenny also had to share a bedroom with Rachel until Jenny finally left for college. So Jenny is the one who taught Rachel to keep her room clean. Jenny taught Rachel to read scriptures every night. Jenny taught Rachel to pray always. I tried teaching Rachel those things too, but Rachel only rolled her eyes at me. Jenny was her daily example.

I tried to teach Rachel math, but it was a total disaster. Jenny stepped in to not only save Rachel from me, but to teach her algebra and calculus. I tried to teach Rachel sewing, which was another total disaster; I finally succeeded only because Jenny wasn't there to save her. But I couldn't teach her to like it.

I tried to teach Rachel to cook, but who's kidding whom? I really can't cook. Now that Rachel is in college and actually cares about cooking, she calls Jenny with her cooking questions. Can I help it if my rhubarb pie turned out more like rhubarb pudding-something?

Yet, I still claim that I raised Rachel. I'm just not sure why I claim that. Oh, wait, I know—it's because I'm the one who sits staring out the window wondering what Rachel's up to when she's been gone for two semesters. It's because I'm the one who calls and says, "So, what are your plans for employment this summer?" It's because I'm the one who says, "Yes, we'd all like a new car—and your summer job is what?" It's because I'm the one who calls and says, "Whatever you do, don't call Dad this week—he just got your cell phone bill. You might want to give him a few days."

I also make this claim because I'm the one who cried when she got on the bus for her first day of kindergarten. I'm the one who cried at her graduation. I'm the one who cried when she left for college. And I'll be the one to cry at her wedding (and pay for it). Yes, no matter what her sister says, I'm the one who cries for Rachel; therefore, I am the mother.

Jenny definitely understands mothering, though. She called me a few short weeks after the birth of her third son. It was Mother's Day. I think her comment was something like, "Only a man would have established Mother's Day on a Sunday." I think she meant that getting three little boys and a husband ready for church, keeping them all quiet for three hours, coming home quickly to change clothes before flying off to her in-laws for a celebratory dinner (with salads in tow, of course), and then rushing back home again—all with a three-week-old baby—was just too much for one woman. She was exhausted and wondered which part of her day she was supposed to enjoy.

Why do we volunteer to do something so exhausting and still try to maintain our sanity? Because it's when we women wear "the mothering hat" that we come closest to charity—the pure love of Christ. I try to love my neighbors. I try to love my enemies. I even tried to love the guy who stole a seat from me at the state track meet. But it's when I'm loving in a mothering capacity that I come the closest to true charity. I think that is when my intent is the purest.

Just to set the record straight, I lost. Jenny won. She is Rachel's mother. Let's face it—she's also *my* mother most of the time. I called Rachel the other day at college; I told her she needed to stay with Jenny when she came home for the weekend. I had an open house to prepare for, and I just didn't need Rachel's little piles of "stuff" where I knew she'd drop them all over the house. I knew Rachel would do all I asked of her, but I knew she'd do it at her own pace. She wouldn't get up until nine, and she'd need an hour to eat breakfast and another hour to "get ready" to help me. Then she'd have to spend two hours on the phone with friends before I could depend on her help. Our styles are so different that I just didn't have the leisure to be her mother on that particular weekend. But Jenny did.

Jenny is just better at the whole charity issue than I am, and I have to work a lot harder at it than she does. I admit it, she's the better mother. But what can I say . . . she had a great teacher.

If It Stretches, It Counts

Stretching—whether it's in spiritual matters, in physical matters, or in our ability to serve others—can sometimes be difficult, but it results in our ability to eventually grow. The goals you set in these areas will, therefore, bring as much growth and development as the effort you invest. But don't let that discourage you, especially if you have a hard time at first coming up with items to fit into each category.

You might be surprised, for example, how easy it is to maintain a "Something Physical" goal. Almost anything that requires movement or improving health can be counted. Okay, not anything. Anything beyond your normal routine would count. Switching loads of laundry doesn't count. But vacuuming the drapes might count—as would taking down the curtains, washing them, and re-hanging them.

Washing the dishes? Probably doesn't count. But washing the walls for spring cleaning definitely counts. Raking leaves in the fall counts, as does cleaning rain gutters, rearranging the storage room, canning, and cleaning out the spud cellar.

Flying a kite in the spring counts. Catching a frog for the boys counts. If you get dressed up in a swimming suit and play for ten minutes on the kids' slippy-slide, it will definitely count. If you let me know about it, I'll send you a Get Out of Jail Free card. If you call me so that I can watch, we could both count it.

Anything that is not routine (and let's *hope* the slippy-slide isn't your routine) counts. Here's the problem: we like routine. It doesn't stretch us. It doesn't interfere with our TV shows or our hobbies or our social lives. Okay, I have no social life; I just threw that in, in case one of you still has one. But let's be realistic: if you're the slippy-slide type, you killed your social life a long time ago without any help from me.

Another aspect of "Something Physical" is changing a diet to increase good health. Cooking healthier counts. Drinking more water counts. For me, a massage and a little relaxing music bring definite physical benefits and seem to interrupt my headache cycle.

In fact, relaxing and breaking out of a rut count, too. I went to a ward Halloween party last year and saw several adult women dressed in the greatest costumes—Super Woman, hula girls, witches, biker babes. Then there were women like me who sat in a corner and tried to stay out of the way. I noticed something. I noticed that the women dressed in costumes looked far less stressed than those of us who did not dress up—they were freer to laugh and freer to let go of their worries. I decided right then and there that next year I would wear a costume, and that would count for a physical goal. These kinds of things don't replace physical exercise, but they can certainly enhance it.

When I list my physical goals, I'm even going to count taking the time out to give myself a facial. What will you count?

Keeping the "Something Spiritual" goal may be a stretch for some. For others, it won't. Hopefully you already study your scriptures and pray; if not, this is a good time to start. Preparing for family home evening or making little family home evening lessons for young families fits in there somewhere.

Adding to a list of things you're grateful for counts as a spiritual activity. Family history work, temple attendance, fasting, preparing for Primary sharing time, reading conference addresses, or watching reruns of conference addresses all work for this goal too.

I love attending BYU-Idaho's Education Week each summer. Meditating about all the things I learn there fills my spiritual goal for several days. Walking from class to class fills my physical goals for those particular four days—and massaging my aching legs for the next week is also something physical that extends the benefit. I highly recommend taking classes there, at BYU Education Week, or at any LDS Institute of Religion. Memorizing scriptures is another good way to stretch yourself and achieve a spiritual goal. The tune to "Eensy Weensy Spider" fits nicely with 2 Nephi 32:3, and "Little White Duck" fits with Helaman 5:12 if you add a refrain to the end. At the moment I'm working on D&C 18:10 and 15–16. I've found that if you just speak the first verse, the rest will fit with "Little Purple Pansies." It's a very cool way to learn scriptures.

I personally struggle more with the "Something of Service" category than with the other two. My struggle comes in stretching myself consistently. It's easy enough to fix a funeral salad five or six times a year or to go visiting teaching once a month. But what about the other twenty-nine days of the month? I refuse to count laundry and cooking as service, because I have to do those things for myself anyway. On days when I'm desperate I guess I can count them, but it feels like cheating. I hate that feeling—it feels like my expectations were too low.

There are days when I simply forget to make a conscious decision to serve. It takes some training and discipline to ask myself every single day what I can do for someone else. Sometimes just being polite is a stretch for me. Sometimes not complaining to my husband is a stretch—and that's certainly a service to him. Today I tried to keep my nose out of my son-in-law's work schedule, and it *would have been* a service if I'd been able to do it. It's a good thing it's only six thirty in the evening—I still have a few hours to fit something in. Maybe I can zip an email to a friend.

But I will try again tomorrow. I will try to do something spiritual, something physical, and something of service. I hope you will try, too. If Aunt Mae can do it at seventy-six, then we can do it. Let's set our goals. Let's stretch ourselves. Sisters, let's not be blind. Let's develop the vision to see eternity.